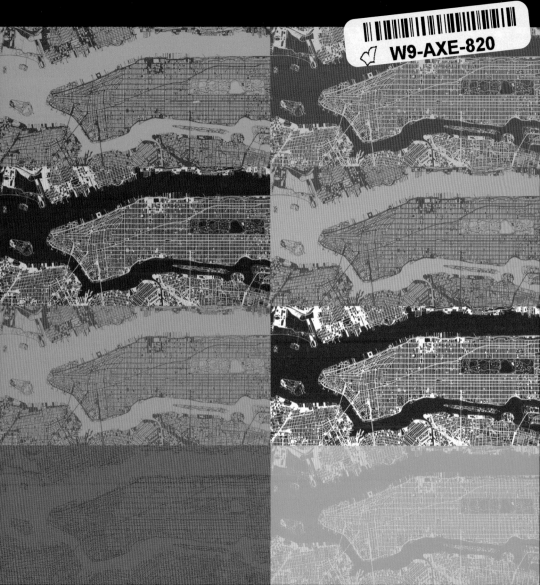

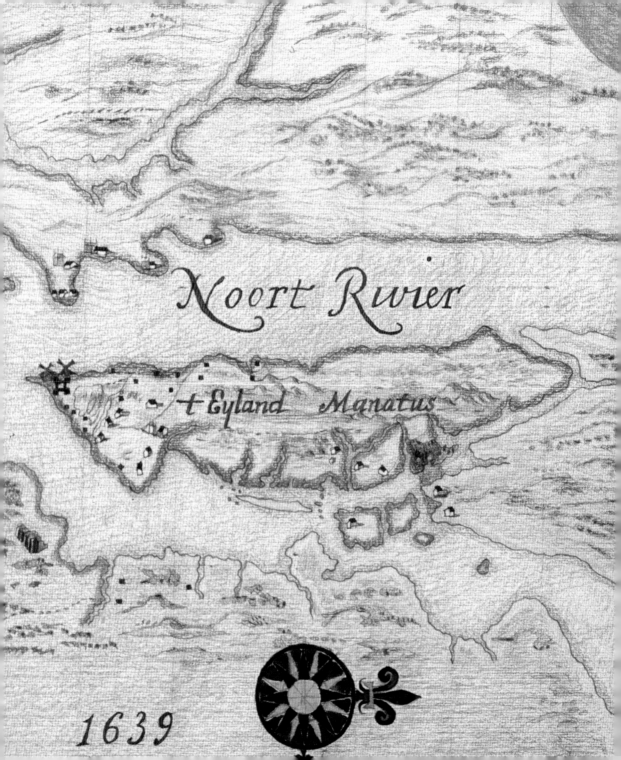

Noort Rivier

't Eyland Manatus

1639

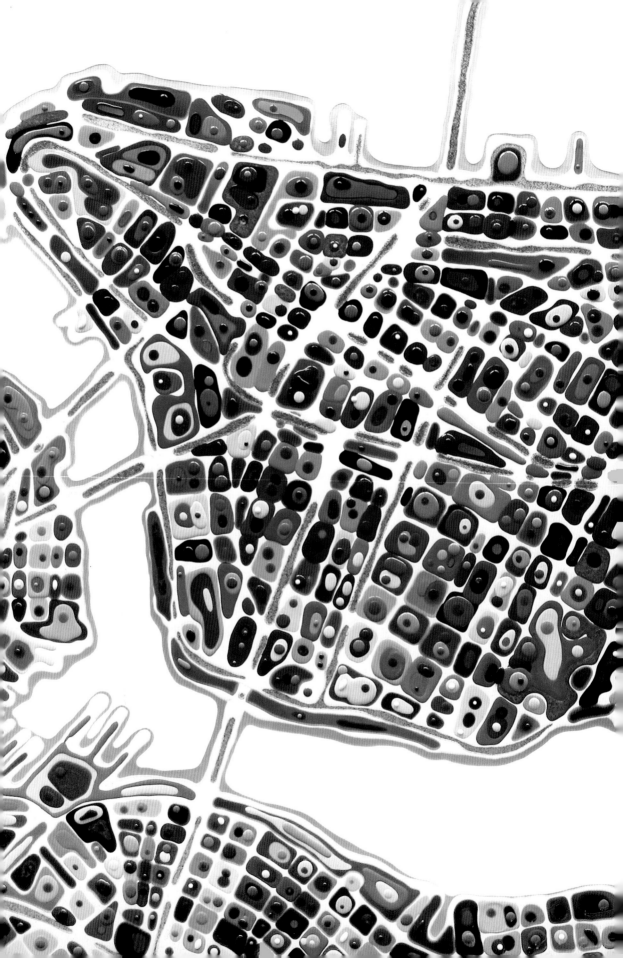

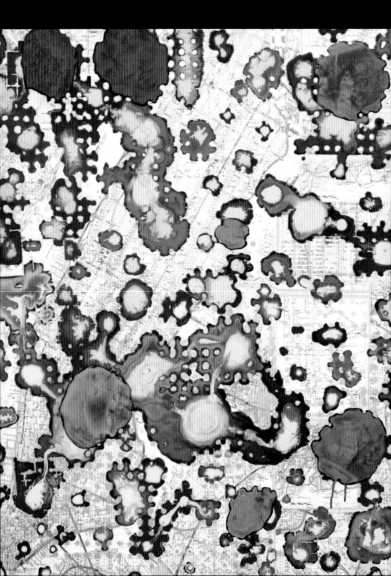

YOU ARE HERE

MAPPING THE SOUL
OF THE CITY

Katharine Harmon

PRINCETON ARCHITECTURAL PRESS · NEW YORK

CONTENTS

KLARI REIS

Manhattan Blue (detail), 2012
40 x 40 in.

Manhattan White (detail), 2012
48 x 72 in.

From a series, *Street Anatomy*
Mixed media on floating aluminum panel

Klari Reis marries biology and technology in her art, exploring the natural by way of the unnatural. Her medium of choice is epoxy polymer, an ultra-glossy, UV-resistant plastic similar to resin, which she pigments with oils, acrylics, powders, and industrial dyes. She compares her studio to a laboratory, where she experiments with the many properties of this challenging material—wearing a Tyvek suit and a respirator, and wielding tools such as a blowtorch, a hair dryer, and pipettes. Upon seeing her own cells under a microscope during an illness, Reis became intrigued by how cells develop and mutate. The cellular forms in her urban maps suggest biological systems of cities, continually morphing in a giant metropolitan petri dish.

CHRISTINE GURTLER

Color Grid of New York (detail), 2012
Acrylic overlaid with hand-cut mat
18 x 18 in.

While studying at Parsons School of Design, Christine Gurtler created this piece for a color theory class. The assignment was to paint a creative color wheel. She chose to depict a section of Manhattan, with Union Square at center, as a study of hue and tone. She overlaid this with a hand-cut mat to add dimension while indicating the map's streets. Gurtler is currently the design director for a New York–based design firm.

PLANOS URBANOS

NY 4 x 2, 2014
Giclée print of computer-generated art
20 x 20 in.

Several years ago a duo of Spanish architects—Jasone Ayerbe and Javier R. Recco—took up creative mapping on the side, under the name Planos Urbanos. They are interested in the aesthetics of mapping, reviving—in their words—"something lost in cartography since the mid-20th century." They feel that while mapping has refined a set of universal codes readable in different languages and cultures, it can emphasize creative values, too. "Since we started working on mapping," they write, "we learned that representation of reality should have an artistic component alongside with a scientific base."

NY 4 x 2 is an homage to Andy Warhol and New York; the artists note the impossibility of Warhol without the city and the city without Warhol. (It is thus fitting that this book ends with a map by Warhol.)

JOYCE KOZLOFF

Stars Over Manhattan I
(Noort River, 1639), 2002
Mixed media on paper
11¾ x 21½ in. each
Private collection
Courtesy DC Moore Gallery, New York

This conceptual drawing depicts one of four murals Joyce Kozloff proposed for the subway station at 86th Street and Lexington. Each mural was split between a terrestrial and a celestial map. This piece paired a 1639 Dutch map with a fanciful detail of the northern night sky as depicted in an English cartograph published in 1790. Kozloff's rich exploration of mapping spanning decades includes a selection of NYC artworks, such as a poster showing streets in Manhattan, Queens, and Brooklyn named after Jewish women (such as, in a section of Chelsea, Goldie Hawn Street in place of 14th, Lillian Ross Street in place of 16th, and Linda McCartney for 18th).

CRISTINA BARROSO

Poet, 2009
Acrylic, shellac, map mounted on canvas
39½ x 31½ in.
Private collection Stuttgart

Cristina Barroso has lived in Berlin, San Francisco, Milan, Stuttgart, Los Angeles, and São Paulo, and has used maps as inspiration and material in the rich body of paintings, drawings, and objects she has created over a twenty-five-year career. *Poet* shows Manhattan and boroughs as if viewed from a satellite, with layers of vibrant clouds obscuring what might be realities of life on the ground.

NINA KATCHADOURIAN

Hand-held Subway, 1996
Cibachrome
13 x 19 inches

Nina Katchadourian works in a number of artistic fields, including photography, sculpture, sound, video, curation, and teaching. Over the course of a year, during walks through Manhattan and Brooklyn, she collected lengths of cassette tape she found on the ground, snarled in trees, and caught in subway grates. She mapped their

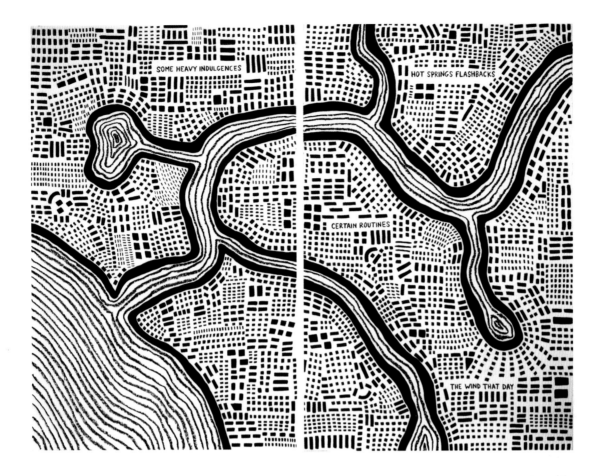

locations and compiled clips of these audio gleanings to create a unique mixtape of the city. Around the same time, Katchadourian was inspired to dissect a map of the New York subway system; it looks like a tangle of audio tape, its content similarly obscured. With form disguising function, the map becomes just another handful of urban flotsam.

PAGE 8

MARK ULRIKSEN
Center of the Universe, 1999
Acrylic on paper
16 x 12 in. each

Mark Ulriksen is an artist and widely published illustrator who, as of press time, has contributed over fifty covers to the *New Yorker.* This is number thirteen, inspired by a photo of the Milky Way he saw while thumbing through a favorite book, *The Bettman Portable Archive.* He thought, "Ah, the center of the universe. Exactly how New Yorkers perceive themselves. That might make a good cover." It did, on January 10th, 2000.

TOP

DAHLIA ELSAYED
Some Heavy Indulgences, 2009
Acrylic and oil stick on paper
40 x 26 in. each

Dahlia Elsayed combines text and imagery in narrative paintings that document internal and external geographies. Her work, influenced by conceptual art, comics, and landscape painting, are illustrations of place and experience. A native New Yorker, Elsayed often tracks emotional and sensory states of life in the metropolitan area. She uses a diaristic format to create a visual record of autobiographical events mixed with external data of weather, navigation, and ephemeral encounters, particularly around the Hudson River (which she crosses repeatedly by bike, foot, car, bus, and ferry).

I am sitting at the moment in a stifling hotel room in 90-degree heat,

halfway down an air-shaft, in midtown. No air moves in or out of the room,

yet I am curiously affected by emanations from the immediate surroundings.

I am twenty-two blocks from where Rudolph Valentino lay in state,

eight blocks from where Nathan Hale was executed, five blocks

from the publisher's office where Ernest Hemingway hit Max Eastman

on the nose, four miles from where Walt Whitman sat sweating out editorials

for the *Brooklyn Eagle*, thirty-four blocks from the street Willa Cather lived in

when she came to New York to write books about Nebraska, one block

from where Marceline used to clown on the boards of the Hippodrome,

thirty-six blocks from the spot where the historian Joe Gould kicked a radio

to pieces in full view of the public, thirteen blocks from where Harry Thaw shot

Stanford White, five blocks from where I used to usher at the Metropolitan Opera

and only a hundred and twelve blocks from the spot where Clarence Day

the Elder was washed of his sins in the Church of the Epiphany

(I could continue this list indefinitely); and for that matter I am probably

occupying the very room that any number of exalted and somewise

memorable characters sat in, some of them on hot, breathless afternoons,

lonely and private and full of their own sense of emanations from without.

—E. B. White, *Here Is New York,* 1949

INTRODUCTION

At the beginning of his masterful, oft-quoted essay *Here Is New York*, E. B. White creates a perfect map. We can triangulate his location, the "I am here" dot he has pinned in midtown Manhattan (in today's precise terms, 40° 45′ 21.4″ N 73° 58′ 56.8″ W, or a room in the Algonquin Hotel)—but White's word map is about stories. It thrums with "the vibrations of great times and tall deeds, of queer people and events and undertakings." It conveys the intensity of a colossal city and the passions of millions of souls who have claimed a piece of it. White beautifully illustrates that in New York there is so very, very much to map.

What is it about the city that invites mapping? First, perhaps, is a need to find one's place here. An endlessly morphing population of contemporary lives humming along, side by side and mutually oblivious, feeds a need to locate oneself. Another *New Yorker* writer, A. J. Liebling, wrote in 1938 of the city's multiplicity of lives: "the worlds of weight lifters, yodelers, tugboat captains, and sideshow barkers, of the book ditchers, sparring partners, song pluggers, sporting girls and religious painters, of the dealers in rhesus monkeys and the bishops of churches." Diversity fills the city with cartographic potential. Density, ethnicity, race, heritage, languages, income differentials, locals versus commuters versus tourists—all can be, and have been, mapped. New York belongs to everyone, and maps prove it.

One of the city's greatest charms is that it looms large enough for all. Everywhere in the world people know New York, whether or not they've visited, and if pressed many could draw a mind's-eye map of it—perhaps of Manhattan in profile, spiky with skyscrapers and lit up like Times Square, or the entire city from above, boroughs dotted with film crews capturing mad car chases and NYPD teams investigating heinous crimes. The city is a media celebrity, inviting our projections. When I first visited New York as a child, I was in for a surprise. Skyscrapers didn't cover all of Manhattan and the boroughs, and the Statue of Liberty wasn't towering head and shoulders over them all.

New York's enduring icons, both physical and conceptual, anchor its maps. A deep repository of historical documents provides base maps for illustrating flux. The familiar subway map—a graphic synonym for the city—is ready for riffing, and Manhattan's street grid offers another visual trope. While most city maps focus on frenzied Manhattan, the boroughs offer other experiences and locations for cartographic exploration. New York stereotypes bring forth humorous maps; its excesses prompt sarcastic maps; its profusion of imagery

ANONYMOUS

Map of New York World's Fair 1939 and Metropolitan Area, c.1939
Color process print
40 x 40 in.
Courtesy George Glazer Gallery

inspires artists' maps. The city as cartography is never more evident than when seen from on high. From the sixty-ninth floor of the Top of the Rock, or the eighty-sixth floor of the Empire State Building, you can find maps in every direction of the compass rose scrolling out from beneath your feet.

∽

Do a bit of web diving and you'll discover an exuberance of New York cartography: maps of alien sightings in the city; a mapped comparison of the numbers of zombies and vampires (way more vampires); where the city gets most kinky, and where Manhattan's rich, single men are; the places you're most likely to see celebrities; the locations of sitcoms; the best sledding hills; the best places to nap. Some couldn't get any more specific: a map of which community gardens grow collard greens, for example, and a map of restaurants with lamb chops on the menu (in case the apocalypse looms, the map's creators explain, and you crave lamb chops for your last good meal). You can find maps of Manhattan's most common dog breeds and dog names, by neighborhood, and a map of neighborhoods with the most dog poop. A rock 'n' roll map of Manhattan pinpoints the locations of Patti Smith's "Birdland" and Lou Reed's "Halloween Parade," "Hyperstation" by Sonic Youth and "Famous Blue Raincoat" by Leonard Cohen. Numerous maps show Marvel superheroes' bases of operation and the lairs of their foes, and Batman's Gotham City, and Superman's Metropolis. And if you long for a Super Mario version of the subway map, it exists. Several versions, in fact.

Cartographic artists use all manner of materials. There are New York woodcut maps, knitted maps, embroidered maps framed by doilies, gilded maps, and a map of the boroughs made of honeycomb (page 53). The artist Katarina Jerinic mapped a mountain range of snowbanks in Crown Heights. Other artists have created an eighty-foot Day-Glo map of Manhattan, a map constructed of Lego bricks, and a tiny, delicate map made from crushed eggshells.

Now is the age of the citizen mapper, and New York does not lack for creative geo-visualizers. Infographic maps abound. Curious about city property? Find maps of values, ages and heights of buildings, foreclosures, and where land has been seized by eminent domain. Fueling unease are crime maps, incarceration maps, rat maps, hurricane evacuation maps, climate change maps. There are maps of what New Yorkers complain about (mostly garbage, vermin, noise, graffiti, and blown-out streetlights, the order depending on the neighborhood) and maps of happiness,

too. For example, a 2011 map based on software analysis of New Yorkers' tweeted emoticons shows the most positive vibes around Central Park (and a locus of negativity around Maspeth Creek's smelly Superfund site). A 2012 mood map based on data from Wyst, a "social discovery" app, identifies SoHo as the happiest neighborhood and Greenpoint the most fun (while the Financial District is the angriest, and Clinton Hill the saddest).

But information-laden maps go only so far. Fortunately, New York has no shortage of artists ready to explore its psychogeographical terrain. The city is exhilarating and exhausting, frustrating and fulfilling, alienating and embracing. Artists mapping emotional experiences encounter an apparent contradiction: the notion that New Yorkers become inured to heightened levels of stimulus in order to maintain mental equilibrium; and that life in the city may elicit a more intense range and depth of emotional expression in its residents as compared with those of other, calmer locales. New York offers creative wayfinders a many-faceted urban psyche to explore. With so many facets, and such a healthy ego, the city seems to leave little mappable territory beyond its borders (opposite).

In doing the research for *You Are Here NYC*, I compiled a database of more than a thousand maps, and finally had to make myself stop cataloging and start choosing. The two hundred maps in this book combine compelling content with visual appeal, and fall into six categories: the city's development, neighborhood life, transportation modes, cultural terrain, personal geographies, and ability to inspire awe. The question I asked with each choice was: does this map have the potential to intrigue even the most jaded of New Yorkers, or at least stir their pride? Happily, both conceptually and aesthetically, city mappers cleared that bar again and again. Essay contributors explore the city's genius for inspiring cartography, discussing several of the most iconic New York maps—Saul Steinberg's *The View from Ninth Avenue* (pages 46–47), the *Panorama of the City of New York* (pages 24–25), and *New Yorkistan* by Maira Kalman and Rick Meyerowitz (pages 118–21)—and map types, including pictorial maps, walking maps, and maps of scents.

My favorite maps have a touch of whimsy. The density

ANONYMOUS
New York, 1970
Print on paper
24 x 20 in.
Courtesy David Rumsey Historical Map Collection

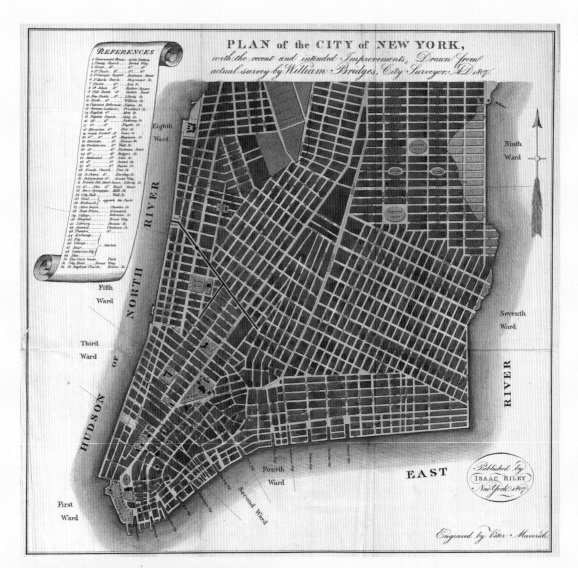

PLAN of the CITY of NEW YORK,
with the recent and intended Improvements. Drawn from
actual survey by William Bridges, City Surveyor, AD 1807.

WILLIAM BRIDGES

Plan of the City of New York, with the Recent and Intended Improvements, 1807, from *Manual of the Corporation of New York,* 1871
Courtesy Geographicus Rare Antique Maps, via Wikimedia Commons

LEFT

CHARLES-ANTOINE PERRAULT

New York/Paris Mashup: Manhattan's Grid Revisited, 2011
Digitally generated image

of Manhattan and the value of its real estate have inspired numerous unrealized plans for the island's expansion (see essay on pages 72–75). To my delight, I found a map by a cartographer, William Bridges, who chose to skip the bother of all that earth-moving; he simply went ahead and expanded the map. In 1807 Bridges was the city's surveyor, and he produced a map intended for visitors that included a gridded, angular extension of Manhattan's southeast side (left). The map's "intended improvements" included new streets that would have sent muddled tourists deep into the East River. Another whimsical map, by Charles-Antoine Perrault, imagines Manhattan with a Parisian street design (page 16, bottom). It begs the question: would Manhattan have a different character without its grid?

And what would the city be if Manhattan went AWOL? In 1975 Robert Grosvenor conceived of relocating the island as a means for reclaiming it (below). The plan involved freeing the island by blasting, removing the bedrock beneath, attaching a flotation collar, and testing it for seaworthiness. Grosvenor left open the question of where it would be towed—or if it would be set adrift as a sovereign piece of flotsam. Along similar lines, the demographic cartographer Bill Rankin was inspired by Rem Koolhaas's floating pool

project to create *The Errant Isle of Manhattan*, a series of fun mash-ups showing the island docked in various cities, such as in Lake Michigan alongside Chicago, or nosing into the Delaware River next to Philadelphia. "I wondered what would happen if Manhattan…decided to take a tour of the oceans," Rankin wrote, "stopping at other cities to refuel and have a good time. Overwhelmed by Los Angeles's vastness, Manhattan decides to stay offshore, while it snuggles in close and completely overwhelms Boston (and inadvertently obliterates Logan airport)."

For interactive conceptual artists using maps as a means rather than an end (or both means and end), New York proffers serendipitous rewards. Three examples: Yumi Roth asks random people to suggest places to go, and has them draw maps to these locations on her hand. She then uses the maps to ask for directions from others, making the map an intermediary among strangers (page 131). Nobutaka Aozaki, a Japanese artist based in New York, is building a geographic mosaic of hand-drawn maps that he has gathered from random street encounters. Disguised as a tourist (with a souvenir NYC baseball cap, backpack, and Century 21 shopping bag), Aozaki asks strangers to draw maps on available scraps of paper directing him to various locations drawn as maps

ROBERT GROSVENOR
Removal of Manhattan Island, 1975
Courtesy Paula Cooper Gallery

NOBUTAKA AOZAKI

From Here to There (Manhattan), 2012–ongoing
Map assemblage (detail): ink, paper, map pins
132 x 60 in. (to date)
Photo documentation by Yuriko Katori

on scraps of paper. Piece by piece, he is assembling a map of Manhattan (opposite). He sees the collaborative project as documentation of a disappearing form of communication: a wayfinding map that doesn't involve a smartphone. For a Whitney Museum education program, the counter-cartographer Lize Mogel led a group of teens in creating nonconventional "deep maps" of the Meatpacking District that explore personal relationships with place, using idiosyncratic themes such as the boundaries of cobblestone streets, coffee shops that aren't Starbucks, and doors without doorknobs.

Looking around, you'll quickly find your own New York to map. There are many ways to get in the mood. For example, for those with time on their hands, the New York Public Library's online Map Warper is a wonderfully addictive "georectification" tool that enables you to align historic and contemporary maps in the library's collection, thereby helping to build a city of maps. Or visit the library in person and check out its extensive map collection. Or, back online, play with Smithsonian.com's interactive double-map—an 1836 carto-graphic lens you can drag atop a current photograph (right). Or head to Rockefeller Center to see what abstraction can do for historical mapping, on a grand scale, in Mark Bradford's *Elgin Gardens* (following pages).

Or you can follow the lead of the famed artist Sol LeWitt, who in the seventies made a number of *100$ Drawings* con-sisting of black-and-white satellite images of cities with geo-graphical features, or geometric chunks, excised. For example, his New York series included *Photo of Part of Manhattan with the Area Between 117 Hester St, 420 W. Broadway and Morty's Liquor Store Cut Out,* and *Manhattan with Roosevelt Island Removed.* The titles were instructions anyone could use to replicate the works—in keeping with LeWitt's interest in the decommodification of art, and as a wink at any belief in maps' reliability. Go ahead and create your very own LeWitt. Remove anything you like—or anything you don't. Or cut out a chunk of the map as a special gift to a friend (right).

New York has no shortage of inventive thinkers who make excellent cartographers. Each act of creative cartography reflects both the state of mind of the mapper and the state of the city. And each contributes another page to a giant, ever-accumulating atlas of New York—an atlas as big as the city's self-regard. Perhaps, in the end, what makes the city the most mapped metropolis in the world is that it offers com-plete cartographic liberty. In New York, nothing is to scale.

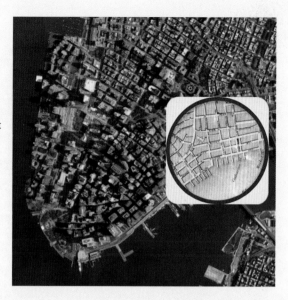

Interactive feature with historic map on photograph
From Smithsonian.com
Historic map from David Rumsey Map Collection
Interactive courtesy of Esri

SOL LEWITT
A Triangle of Manhattan for Arlan, 1979
Cut silver gelatin print
7⅞ x 15½ in.
Courtesy James Cohan Gallery

MARK BRADFORD

Elgin Gardens, 2015
Mixed media on canvas
Two parts, 253½ x 253½ in. each
Courtesy the artist and Hauser & Wirth
Photos by Josh White

Bradford created this colossal pair of paintings, each twenty-one feet square, for the lobby of Rockefeller Center's 1221 Avenue of the Americas. Working from an early map of the city's grid, the L.A. artist covered the canvases (lower Manhattan, left, and upper Manhattan, right) with successive latticeworks of rectangular shapes reminiscent of blocks, buildings, lots, and fields.

The work's title alludes to one of the property's historical layers. At the beginning of the 18th century, Dr. David Hosack, a prominent New York physician, purchased nearly

twenty acres of city common pasture lands (the equivalent of four city blocks) around the site of today's Rockefeller Center. There he established the Elgin Botanic Gardens, primarily for the study of therapeutic plants by medical students and doctors. The property had a greenhouse, two hothouses, a pond, and two thousand plant species. It was later sold to the state, and thereafter fell into neglect. In 1857 the first portion of the property was sold for development, and eighty years later John D. Rockefeller Jr. built "the city within a city"—the complex of commercial buildings we know today.

A footnote: among many distinctions, Hosack was among the first doctors to use a stethoscope, and to advocate for vaccination against smallpox. He was a founder of the Humane Society, Bellevue Hospital, the New York Horticultural Society, and the New-York Historical Society. And perhaps most famously, Hosack was Alexander Hamilton's attending physician at his fatal duel with Aaron Burr.

A PANORAMA OF POWER *Maria Popova*

"A poem," E. B. White wrote in his 1949 masterpiece *Here Is New York*, "compresses much in a small space and adds music, thus heightening its meaning. The city is like poetry." Nothing compresses the city in order to heighten its meaning more palpably than the Panorama of the City of New York—an astonishing feat of architecture, urban planning, and craftsmanship, strangely poetic in its deliberate contrast of scale and significance. To look at it is to see, perhaps for the first time, a singular city of ordered complexity and elegant enormity, dynamic duality and paradox in action.

Constructed by a team of more than one hundred architectural model builders from Raymond Lester & Associates over the course of three years, this elaborate microcosm reduces every hundred feet of cityscape to one inch of Formica panels and urethane foam. This conceptual compression cost $672,662.69 to construct in 1964—the equivalent of approximately $5 million today. But what makes the Panorama most striking is its affront to our sense of scale. At 9,335 square feet, it is both a miniature and an expanse, containing every street, every park, and every single one of the 895,000 buildings constructed prior to 1992, when Raymond Lester & Associates updated the model.

The Panorama, which now resides at the Queens Museum, was created for the 1964 World's Fair as a celebration of master builder Robert Moses and his indelible imprint on the cityscape. A brilliant architect and a fierce politician who publicly defied politicians—including, in one famous incident, President Franklin D. Roosevelt himself—Moses envisioned and brought to life 658 playgrounds, 416 miles of parkways, 288 tennis courts, 678 baseball diamonds, and numerous major roads and bridges. He was a man animated by "an imagination that leaped unhesitatingly at problems insoluble to other people," as Robert E. Caro wrote in *The Power Broker*, his Pulitzer Prize–winning 1,200-page biography of Moses.

But Moses, like the city itself, was also a man of dualities. Although he began his career as an earnest idealist and an irrepressibly optimistic reformer, the power machine hardened him into a man of "iron will and determination," in Caro's words. Intent on bending the world's greatest city to his will, he imprinted Gotham with his fiery fusion of idealism and egotism. That his legacy should be celebrated by a miniature model of the city, Moses's favorite toy, is only fitting.

Perhaps most emblematic of all is how the Panorama was pitched at the 1964 World's Fair, where it became a favorite attraction as a kind of indoor helicopter tour of the city, promising to provide a "god's-eye view" of the urban ecosystem. In a sense, visitors were invited to try on the view of Moses, a self-anointed god who had drawn the master map not only of the city's infrastructure but also of its very character and destiny—the craftsman of the grand stage onto which, in the immortal words of White, "enormous and violent and wonderful events…are taking place every minute."

❧

Maria Popova is a reader and writer, and writes about what she reads on Brain Pickings *(brainpickings.org), which is included in the Library of Congress archive of culturally valuable materials.*

Panorama of the City of New York,
1961–63
Scale model installation at Queens Museum
9 ⅓ sq. ft.
Courtesy the Queens Museum, photos
by Max Touhey

LIZ HICKOK

Battery Place and Washington Street
From *Fugitive Topography: Jelly NYC,* 2010
Chromogenic print, edition of 12
16 x 30 in. and 30 x 60 in.

LEFT

View from the Staten Island Ferry
Mixed-media sculpture
Dimensions variable

For a 2010 exhibition at Pratt Manhattan Gallery, Liz Hickok spent days constructing an arresting, three-dimensional model of the skyline of Lower Manhattan, evoking both the beauty and the vulnerability of the city. She molded buildings from gel wax, some over a foot tall, transforming skyscrapers into precarious jewels. In Hickok's photographs of the installation, taken from the angle of an approaching immigrant, the cityscape glows with promise; closer in, the buildings slump beneath the weight of so much expectation. The gelatinous medium used for Jelly NYC "takes unexpected turns as it bends, glistens, and melts," says Hickok, "revealing the hidden fragility of the familiar city grid. The buildings assume a human quality as they lean on one another for support." What stories they could tell.

HENRY WELLGE
Greatest New York, 1911
Color lithograph
9 x 27 in.
Lionel Pincus and Princess Firyal Map Division,
New York Public Library

IEW YORK

Henry Wellge was a German-born map artist and publisher who produced more than 150 perspective renderings of small cities, mainly in the Midwest, ranging from Texarkana to Billings, Selma to Duluth. He made this "greatest" map six years before his death in 1917.

Bird's-eye views, also known as illustrated or panorama maps, became a popular cartographic form in the 1840s through the early twentieth century. They offered oblique, aerial vistas as seen from imaginary perspectives—a tricky mapmaking skill, combining an architect's draftsmanship with an artist's aesthetic sensibilities. Currier & Ives and other publishers of the time used the newly developed technology of color lithography to produce affordable prints of thousands of locations in North America.

JOHN BACHMANN

New York and Environs, 1859

Color lithograph

Eno Collection, Miriam and Ira D. Wallach Division of Art, Prints and Photographs,
New York Public Library, Astor, Lenox and Tilden Foundations

John Bachmann, a Swiss-born lithographer, arrived in
the United States in 1848 at the age of thirty-four; that
same year he published his first American perspective map,
looking from Union Square south to lower Manhattan.
Bachmann was an originator of the true bird's-eye view,
a mathematically projected illustration providing a line of
sight from well above the tallest steeples. In his career

Bachmann created many such vistas, and was best
known for those of New York, which made up two-thirds
of his output. He flew much higher than the proverbial
bird for *New York and Environs,* a fish-eye lens on the city.
With its view from directly over New York Harbor, the
waterways of the city are the focus. Governors Island
looms wondrously large.

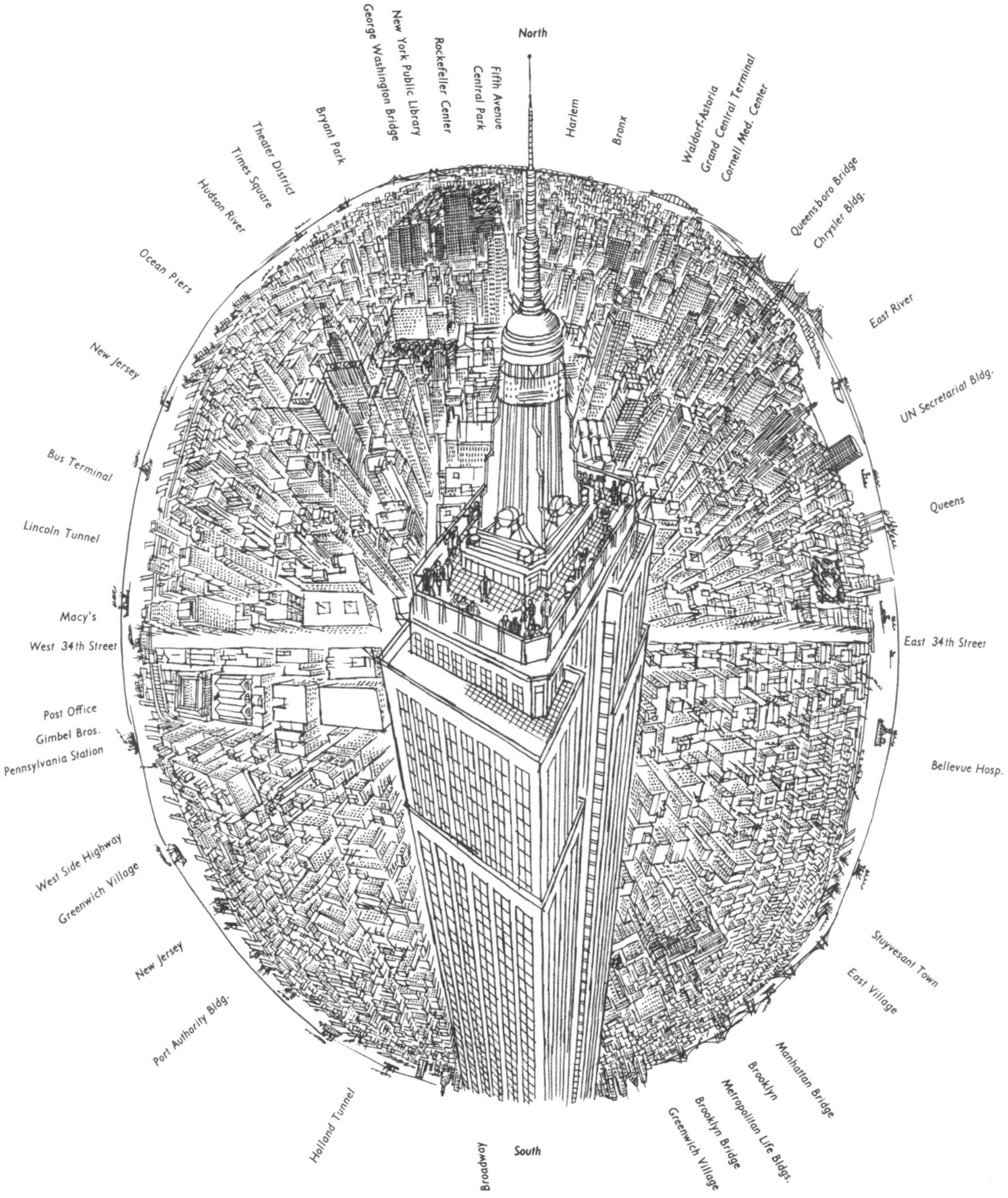
North
Fifth Avenue
Central Park
Rockefeller Center
New York Public Library
George Washington Bridge
Bryant Park
Theater District
Times Square
Hudson River
Ocean Piers
New Jersey
Bus Terminal
Lincoln Tunnel
Macy's
West 34th Street
Post Office
Gimbel Bros.
Pennsylvania Station
West Side Highway
Greenwich Village
New Jersey
Port Authority Bldg.
Holland Tunnel
Broadway
South
Greenwich Village
Brooklyn Bridge
Metropolitan Life Bldgs.
Brooklyn
Manhattan Bridge
East Village
Stuyvesant Town
Bellevue Hosp.
East 34th Street
Queens
UN Secretariat Bldg.
East River
Chrysler Bldg.
Queensboro Bridge
Waldorf-Astoria
Grand Central Terminal
Cornell Med. Center
Bronx
Harlem

ROBINSON

Empire State Panorama

From the book *New York Line by Line*, 1967

Werner Kruse, a German artist who went by the single name Robinson (after Crusoe, which sounds like Kruse), created hundreds of thousands of illustrations in his lifetime. He visited New York in the early 1960s and captured its vibrancy in crowded drawings: people milling about at Grand Central, converging at the doors of St. Patrick's, weaving through cars on Mott Street, or lounging on the steps of the public library. The detailed images, collected in his book *New York Line by Line* (reissued in 2009), are also full of windows by the thousands. Here in this compass map, the artist hovers over the Empire State Building and the surrounding city, parenthetically bordered by the Hudson and East Rivers. Two figures on the observation deck's south-facing corner appear to be looking up at him, about to wave.

G. W. COLTON

Map of the Country Thirty-Three Miles Around the City of New York, 1853
Copper plate engraving
24 x 22 in.
Courtesy David Rumsey Map Collection

In 1777, an anonymous mapper drew the country twenty-five miles around New York, and a meme took hold. By the end of the 1800s, cartographers had published circle-in-a-square charts ranging from twelve to forty miles around the city, including numerous examples created by the Colton family. The maps were most likely used by merchants, professionals, and wealthy travelers. One imagines the journeyers as space explorers tethering themselves to a point at the center of the map before setting out, so that if they ventured beyond its circumference, they could find their way back to Manhattan, the mother ship.

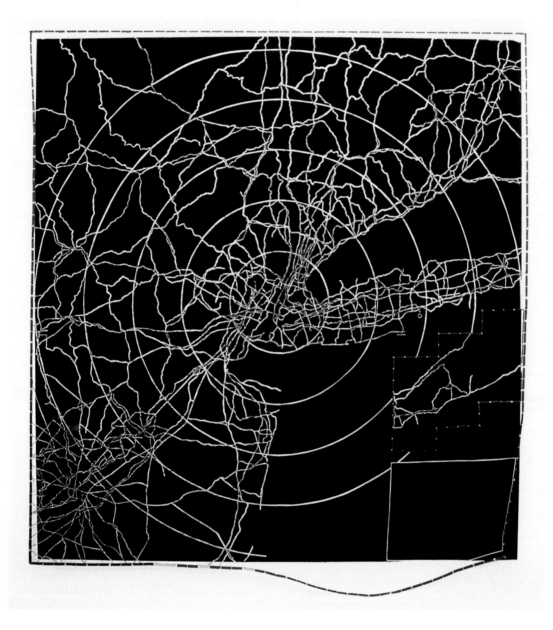

JEFF WOODBURY

Ground Zero, 1999
Dissected map hanging in front of
black square painted on wall
32 x 31 in.

In 1999 Jeff Woodbury dissected a map with Columbus
Circle at its center, radiating out in rings every fifteen miles.
For Woodbury the artwork brought to mind the 1962
fiction best-seller *Fail-Safe*, in which a bomb is dropped on
the Empire State Building; he noted that in many fictional
depictions of nuclear apocalypse, New York is the ultimate
target. A couple of years later, while watching from his
Brooklyn rooftop as the World Trade Center burned and
collapsed, Woodbury thought about the shock waves soon
to radiate from New York around the world.

ELISE ENGLER

Broadway Bridge to West 214th Street

West 50th Street to West 44th Street (Times Square)

Wall Street to Battery Place

From the series, *A Year on Broadway,* 2014–15
Graphite, gouache, colored pencil on paper
Each section 6 x 42½ in.

In her drawings, Elise Engler catalogs aggregated things: everything a fire engine carries, the contents of sixty-five women's purses, all the items in a virology lab. In May 2014 she set out to map the contents of Broadway at street level— its buildings, bushes, bridges, billboards—and neither rain nor snow nor other impediment stayed her from achieving this ambitious feat, completed a year (to the day) later. The connected pieces of the scroll measure nearly 110 feet long, the height of an eleven-story building.

FOLLOWING PAGES

MÉLANIE ELISABETH LEONARD

*A Map of New York in the Air,
or Super-Man-Hattan,* 1928
Color lithograph
24¾ x 35 in.
Courtesy George Glazer Gallery

This may be the only New York map featuring art nouveau styling *and* a purple pterodactyl. And that's not all that makes it special. Map dealer George Glazer surmises that the name "Super-Man-Hattan" reflects the city's forward-thinking, hard-driving, self-reliant ethos—the metropolis as a generator of superiority and success. The map's creator, Massachusetts artist Mélanie Elisabeth Leonard, was perhaps riffing on Friedrich Nietzsche's concept of the Übermensch, popularized in the 1903 George Bernard Shaw play *Man and Superman*. (The not-a-bird, not-a-plane comic book hero did not appear until 1938.)

—Arrogant, the City's beautiful head
   Glows above the swirls of her georgette clouds.
   Below, stark hands grasp Success.
   Drab drays swank thro' the mud:
   Parks gleam greenly. — (Contemporary Poet)

ARANDA/LASCH
The Brooklyn Pigeon Project, 2004
Outdoor installation
With support from the New York State Council for the Arts
Photo above by Peter Hall
Photo below by Reuben for Terraswarm

The rapid development of remote sensing systems and satellite imagery has accustomed us to eye-in-the-sky views of our cities, neighborhoods, and blocks—even our own rooftops. Benjamin Aranda and Chris Lasch attached high-tech wireless cameras to unconventional videographers: pigeons spiraling over Brooklyn, who collected true bird's-eye views. In this experiment with biological satellites, the artists aimed to confront the limits of the GIS grid, thereby creating "an equally rich disclosure of the city: seeing it as a flock does." On their website you can see flight maps and footage featuring Reuben, a handsome, snowy-white videographer with red eye rings.

RIGHT

SOHEI NISHINO

Diorama Map New York, 2006
Light-jet print
68 x 52 in.
Courtesy Michael Hoppen Contemporary

Sohei Nishino, a Japanese artist, walks the streets of a city for weeks, taking thousands of photos from every angle, from high atop skyscrapers down to street level. He makes his own prints from 35mm film, surrounds himself with mounds of photos, and painstakingly arranges them into a sort of memory collage. Although the large, detailed assemblages look like bird's-eye views, each one is a multi-perspective image of a multi-dimensional milieu. Nishino likes subjectivity in maps: "Distance, size—these are such personal things when you think about it," he has said in an interview. "All people perceive them differently. You could say I'm obsessed with finding my own inner scale."

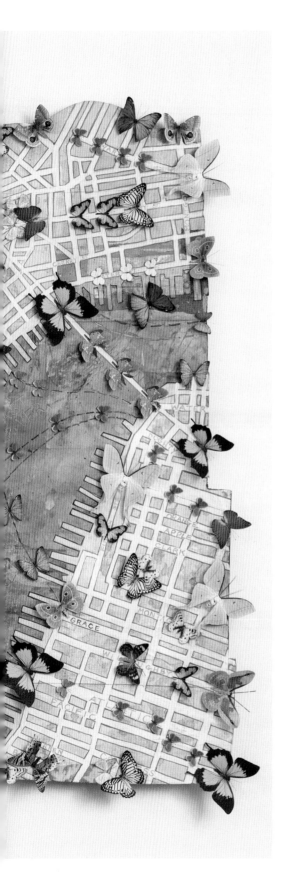

JANE HAMMOND

All Souls (Buttermilk Channel), 2015
Gouache, acrylic, metal leaf, assorted handmade papers,
graphite, colored pencil, archival digital prints, rabbit fur,
feathers, and horsehair
52 x 60 x 3 in.
Courtesy the artist and Galerie Lelong
Collection of the Beekman, a Thompson Hotel, New York

Since 2004 Jane Hammond has made luxuriant maps adorned
with butterflies and moths. The artist focuses on water in this
piece, which is informed by maps from the 1890s, around
the time of the Brooklyn Bridge's construction. She illustrates
a bustling port city where life on the water is as energetic and
congested as it is on land, with flight paths of Lepidoptera
following ferry lines between New Jersey, Manhattan, and
Brooklyn. The migrant species depicted come from all over the
world. Three moths from southern Asia, *Peridrome orbicularis,*
cross the Brooklyn Bridge, led and followed by a Papuan
species, *Papilio ulysses,* a swallowtail named by Carl Linnaeus
for its migratory wanderings. The largest species on the map
is a female atlas moth from the Malay archipelago; Hammond
invented her antennae using peacock crown feathers—the
few tufts standing atop the bird's head. Heading east on
Beaver Street is a North American giant silk moth, *Antheraea
polyphemus,* named for the Cyclops of Greek mythology
because of the "eyes" on its wings. As everyone knows, there
is no shortage of fascinating species in New York.

FOLLOWING PAGES

NILS HANSELL

Wonders of New York, ca. 1953–55
Color lithograph
25 x 33 in.
Courtesy David Rumsey Map Collection

This map is wonder-packed. Into about six square feet Nils
Hansell crammed 301 noteworthy sites, such as 260 Madison,
where redheads run the lifts; the place where Captain Kidd
is believed to have buried treasure; and the venue where
P. T. Barnum displayed a mermaid. He provided insider info
on where to buy almost anything: typewriters, exotic birds, rare
coins, venison and bear, marriage licenses, mounted butterflies,
and much more. In the 1950s in New York one could visit
Barker and Bubbles (seals at the zoo) or the world's largest
cotton exchange, see the daily lineup at police headquarters,
play indoor polo, or hang out in the geographical center of the
Social Register. Hansell conveys well the city's exuberance. He
was a graphic artist known also as the cofounder of Operation
Sail, the parade of "tall ships" on the Hudson River and New
York Harbor that was inaugurated for the 1964 World's Fair and
has recurred once every decade since.

NEW YORK

YUTAKA SONE

Little Manhattan, 2007–09
Marble
33½ x 104½ x 21¾ in.
Courtesy David Zwirner, New York / London

Little Manhattan is three feet tall and nine feet long, and
weighs two and a half tons. Yutaka Sone spent months
walking the city's streets and studying maps and aerial
photographs before spending many more months, with his
assistants, carving the island in exacting detail. Sone says
that the bottom of the sculpture is most important to him.
"I cannot change the shape of Manhattan—or I shouldn't—
but only the top two centimeters are Manhattan," he said
in a 2011 interview. "The top was make, make, make, but
I wanted the bottom to be more poetic and elegant, like
a white feminine dress." Originally trained as an architect,
the Japanese artist is now a sculptor, painter, photographer,
and videographer based in Los Angeles.

HONG SEON JANG

Type City, 2014
Letterpress type on wood
2 x 11 x 14 in.

The New York artist Hong Seon
Jang repurposes familiar objects to
create works exploring structures,
symbols, and patterns. All three
come together in *Type City,* with an
added significance. Like hot type,
New York impresses and leaves its
marks upon the world.

THE VIEW FROM 9TH AVENUE *Bob Mankoff*

When I was asked to do an essay on this, Saul Steinberg's most famous drawing, which then became the most famous, most iconic cover for the *New Yorker* of all time, one that has been rampantly ripped off and pounded by piracy and imitation into a misunderstood cliché of itself, I realized that though I had seen it over and over over the years, I needed to look it over again.

I saw the *New Yorker* cover when it came out in 1976, and it wasn't long before the magazine, in response to popular demand, made it into a poster. And not long after that you could find it on the walls of apartments and college dorms. Soon it was pretty much everywhere, even if only as a local imitation—who knows, maybe even out there on the far right horizon of the drawing, in Russia, perhaps there's a yellowing poster of "The View of the World from Novosibirsk."

At the time the image made its public debut, I was an aspiring *New Yorker* cartoonist, about a year and a half away from publishing my first cartoon in the magazine, and Saul Steinberg, *cartoonist*, was what I aspired to be. Pretty much everything he had drawn, that had been published, I had seen.

But my attitude was like that of the aliens towards the Woody Allen character, Sandy Bates, in *Stardust Memories*. When Bates asks the aliens, "If nothing lasts, why am I bothering to make films, or do anything for that matter?" To which the aliens reply, "We enjoy your films, particularly the early, funny ones."

By the time "View of the World" appeared, Steinberg's work had moved well beyond "the early funny ones" of his "cartoon" phase, epitomized by such books as *All In Line* (1945), and his work for the *New Yorker* in the early and mid fifties. And by 1960, when *The Labyrinth* was published, though Steinberg still used the iconography of the cartoon, as well as any other visual medium that suited his purpose, the purpose was no longer a "gettable" joke. He had crossed the Rubicon from "popular" to "difficult" and would never go back.

The vast popularity of "View of the World" was that it appeared eminently "gettable," especially when the image was topped by the *New Yorker* logo. With that affixed to the image, to put it in New Yorkeese, "what's not to get?"

It seemed to be an unambiguous visualization of that old quote, "If you're leaving New York, you ain't going nowhere."

Yes, it was gettable, and more than that, easily adaptable and therefore adoptable, which is why so many other cities knocked off the cover, to proclaim, however dubiously, under their own local rubric, that *they* were the epicenter of existence. As a born-and-bred New Yawker, my own take was similar, with the very implausibility implicit in the derivative covers' claims, actually making my own native chauvinism seem reasonable in comparison. I mean Novosibirsk may be a nice little city, but gimme a break.

However, once you look at the drawing, and get the cover with its classic *New Yorker*, Rea Irvin font out of your mind, it's clear that provincial pride, no matter how big and self-important the province, is being satirized, not celebrated. To think that everything west of the Hudson is Nowheresville, full of nondescript nothings, is not to be an urbane New Yorker, but an urban bumpkin.

The aforementioned Novosibirsk, for example, has, I'm told, the Novosibirsk Zoo, a world-renowned scientific institution as well as a popular tourist attraction. Should I ever choose to cross the Hudson, I might just go there some day.

∽

Bob Mankoff is the cartoon editor of the New Yorker, *and the author of* How About Never—Is Never Good for You? My Life in Cartoons.

SAUL STEINBERG
View of the World from Ninth Avenue, 1976
Ink, marker, and colored pencil on paper
14 x 11 in.

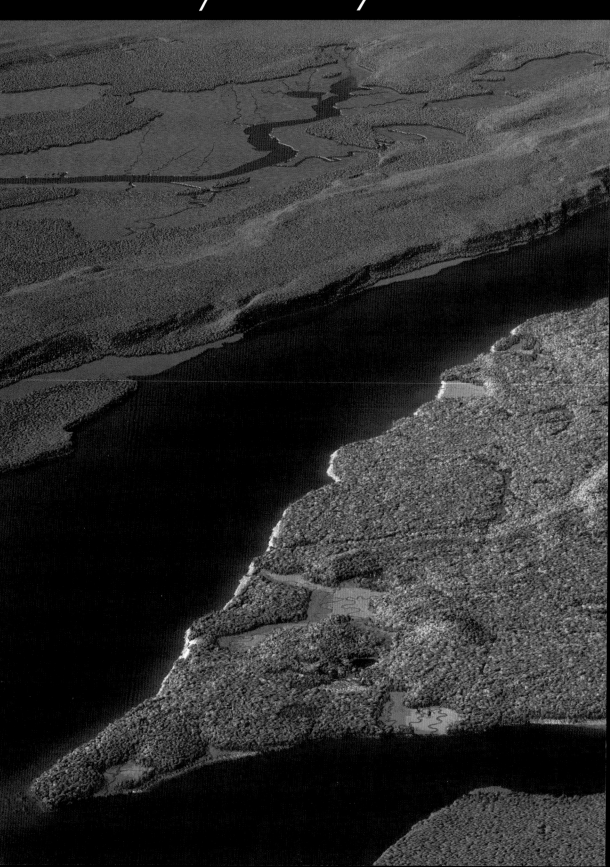

PREVIOUS PAGES

MARKLEY BOYER/
THE MANNAHATTA PROJECT/
WILDLIFE CONSERVATION SOCIETY

Untitled, 2008
Digital reconstruction
60 x 40 in.
Photo by Amiaga Architectural Photography

The Welikia Project is a marvelous
undertaking. It started by providing a look at
Manhattan prior to the arrival of Europeans.
A decade of research revealed the natural
history of Mannahatta (the Lenape name for
the island, meaning "land of many hills"),
an ecologically diverse land mass that for
millennia supported abundant wildlife and
human communities. With a geography
of rises and valleys, forests and meadows,
wetlands and streams, the island was home
to an estimated ten thousand species. Bears,
wolves, and elk once roamed here, no doubt
along with a few mosquitos. The Welikia
("my good home") Project, begun in 2010,
aims to uncover the ecology of New York's
four additional boroughs and the waters
surrounding them.

LEFT

NICHOLAS FRASER
and HEIDI NEILSON

Coastal Oak–Pine Forest

Marine Eelgrass Meadows

Marshy Headwater Stream

From *Forest & Stream,* 2009
Site-specific sidewalk chalk drawings,
14th Street, New York
Each approx. 60 x 84 in.

On an October Sunday in 2009, 14th Street
became a map. At thirty-eight sidewalk sites
between the Hudson and the East River,
chalk-drawn labels identified forest and
wetland sites present in 1609. The labels—
essentially "you are here" markers from four
hundred years ago—were based on data
from the Mannahatta Project. To enhance the
time-warp experience, Heidi Neilson created
a self-guided walking tour, "Urban Forest on
14th Street" (available for download). It's
nice to imagine hiking in an oak-tulip forest at
6th Avenue, or tromping through an eelgrass
meadow at 14th and Avenue C. Wear your
waders.

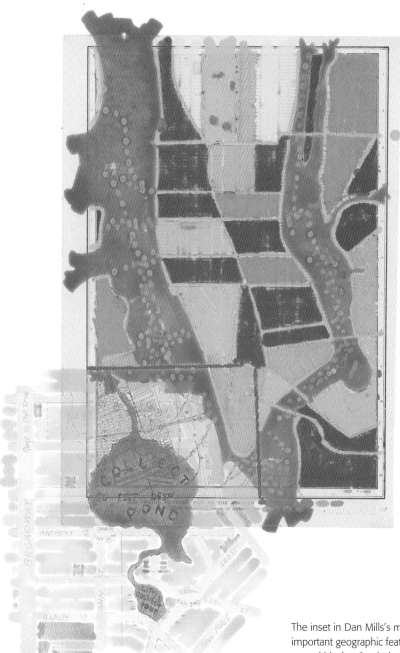

DAN MILLS

New York Excavation II, 2014
Acrylic and graphite on printed map
on paper
30 x 22½ in.

The inset in Dan Mills's map "excavates" an important geographic feature formerly covering several blocks of today's Chinatown. Collect Pond, sixty feet deep and fed by an underground spring, was for two hundred years the main source of water for Manhattan residents. Before that, its shores were—respectively—home to a band of Lenape Native Americans, a popular recreation area for colonists, and a site of polluting slaughterhouses and tanneries. In the early 1800s, to drain what had become an open sewer, engineers built a canal (part of which became Canal Street), yet the area remained for decades a swampy, disease-infested slum. On the site today, Collect Pond Park features a formal reflecting pool perhaps wishing to be a spring-fed pond again.

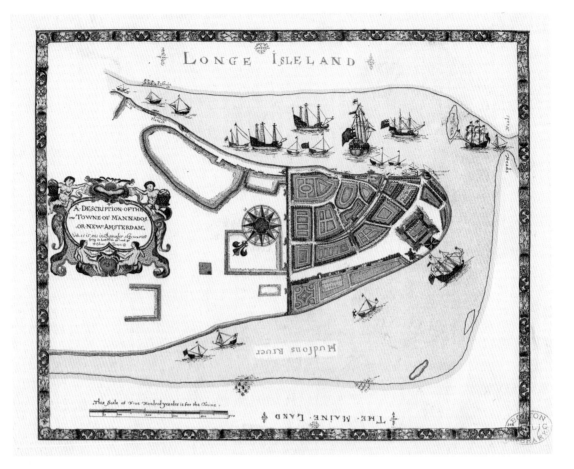

ANONYMOUS

The Duke's Plan of New York: As It Was in September, 1661, Lying in Latitude 40 de. and 40 m., undated
Reproduction of 1664 original, from *A History of the United States and Its People* by Elroy McKendree Avery, 1904
20½ x 26 in.

In 1660 the Dutch surveyor general of New Amsterdam, Jacques Cortelyou, made the earliest extant map of the city (and the only one from the Dutch period), the well-known Castello Plan. Three years later the British captured the colony by order of James Duke of York (later King James II), after whom the city was named. An unknown draftsman, probably in London, prepared for the Duke a more colorful, embellished "plan" of the new British settlement. The future monarch may have been tempted to visit what appears on this map to be a country estate with a large gardening staff. Gone are the buildings and farm plots of the Castello Plan; still visible are the wall at the northern end of the settlement, now Wall Street, and the fort, or battery, now Battery Park. The original of this map is in the British Library, part of the King's Topographical Collection.

LIZ SCRANTON

The Drive of the Hive, 2010
Digital print

On Lopez Island, Washington, Liz Scranton collaborated with honeybees on a New York City mapping project. She carved the subway map's landforms out of honeycomb wired on a specially constructed frame, and inserted it into a hive. In little time, the bees filled the city with brood, nectar, and honey, built comb bridges between the boroughs, and created new property to make way for population growth and greater productivity. Within close confines, literally living on top of each other, hive residents were a model of cooperation, each a part of a remarkable metropolis filled with sweet lucre.

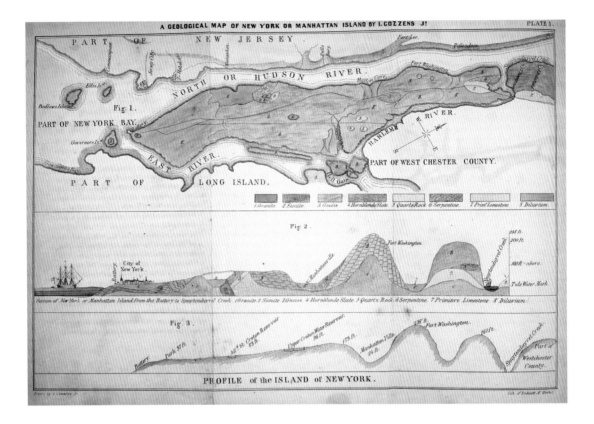

ISSACHAR COZZENS JR.

A Geological Map of New York or Manhattan Island
From the book *A Geological History of Manhattan
or New York Island,* 1843

OPPOSITE

FREDERICK J. H. MERRILL

*Harlem Quadrangle, New York City Folio,
Geologic Atlas of the United States,* 1902
National Geologic Map Database, U.S. Geological Survey

These early geologic maps show—in deceptively soft pastel colors—the rock on which a weighty city rests. The maps are still regarded as mostly accurate, though geologists have refined the rock names and groupings over the past century and a half. Issachar Cozzens Jr.'s map of Manhattan shows surface layers, with islands of bedrock emerging here and there from an orange veneer of sedimentary diluvium. Frederick J. H. Merrill's map shows the deeper, bedrock layers.

The underpinnings of New York are famously durable. The bedrock consists primarily of three types of metamorphic rock: Manhattan schist (in lower and northern Manhattan), Fordham gneiss (primarily in the Bronx), and Inwood marble (in Manhattan and beneath the rivers that surround it). Schist in particular is ideally suited for bearing the weight of skyscrapers. Building heights in Manhattan relate to the depth of the bedrock beneath them; the two concentrations of vertical hyper-development, in Midtown and lower Manhattan, occur where the schist formation is closest to the surface. Outcroppings of schist can be found throughout Manhattan's parks. Perhaps the most arresting example, a massive boulder called Rat Rock, poses for photographs on increasingly valuable real estate between apartment buildings on West 114th Street.

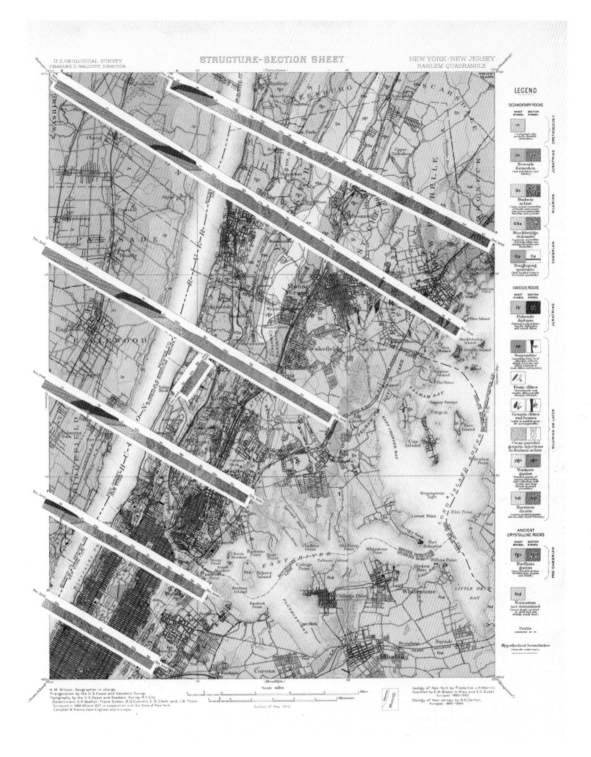

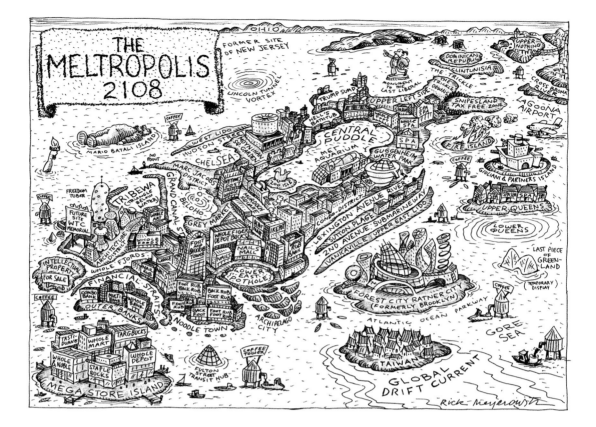

RICK MEYEROWITZ

The Meltropolis 2108, 2008
Ink on paper with graphite overlay
10 x 14 in.

Rick Meyerowitz's projection of life in the city less than a
century from now—made for *Forecast*, the tenth book in the
Nozone series edited by Nicholas Blechman—looks, on the
face of it, pretty sodden. But it won't be all bad, what with
coffee by the boatload, a water park at the Guggenheim, and
plenty of shopping mega-emporiums such as Wholefiger
Depot Bucks. The Last Piece of Greenland (while it lasts) and
the Monument to the Last Liberal will make pleasant boat
tour destinations.

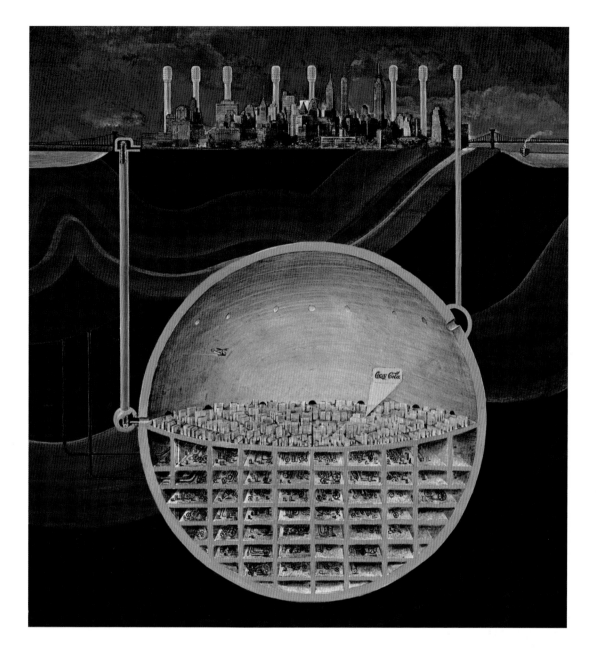

OSCAR NEWMAN

Plan for an underground nuclear shelter (detail)
From *Esquire,* December 1969
Courtesy JF Ptak Science Books

When space in Manhattan gets too tight, here's a recipe for creating a city below it. The New York architect and city planner Oscar Newman proposed in *Esquire* that developers use nuclear explosions to create a colossal underground cavern; build a spherical city within it; erect giant Q-tip-like air filters above; use the dome as a projection screen for advertising Coca-Cola; and there you'd have it, a happy retreat from aboveground realities. Newman presented this plan with tongue firmly in cheek, after learning that an underground atomic test in Nevada had produced just such a hollow subterranean globe. "Manhattan could have half a dozen such atomic cities strung under the city proper," he wrote. "The real problem... in an underground city would be lack of view and fresh air, but consider its easy access to the surface and the fact that, even as things are, our air should be filtered and what most of us see from our windows is someone else's wall."

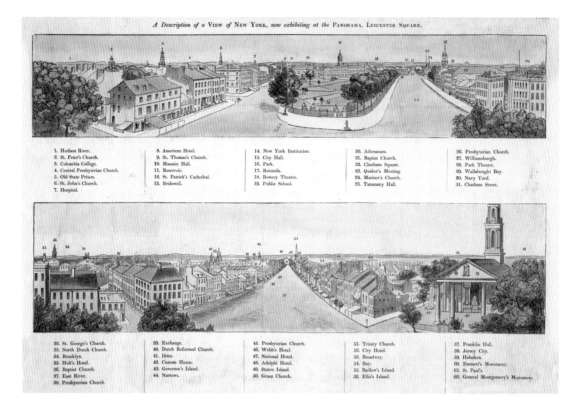

A Description of a View of New York, now exhibiting at the PANORAMA, LEICESTER SQUARE.

1. Hudson River.
2. St. Peter's Church.
3. Columbia College.
4. Central Presbyterian Church.
5. Old State Prison.
6. St. John's Church.
7. Hospital.
8. American Hotel.
9. St. Thomas's Church.
10. Masonic Hall.
11. Reservoir.
12. St. Patrick's Cathedral.
13. Bridewell.
14. New York Institution.
15. City Hall.
16. Park.
17. Rotunda.
18. Bowery Theatre.
19. Public School.
20. Athenæum.
21. Baptist Church.
22. Chatham Square.
23. Quaker's Meeting.
24. Mariner's Church.
25. Tammany Hall.
26. Presbyterian Church.
27. Williamsburgh.
28. Park Theatre.
29. Wallabought Bay.
30. Navy Yard.
31. Chatham Street.

32. St. George's Church.
33. North Dutch Church.
34. Brooklyn.
35. Holt's Hotel.
36. Baptist Church.
37. East River.
38. Presbyterian Church.
39. Exchange.
40. Dutch Reformed Church.
41. Ditto.
42. Custom House.
43. Governor's Island.
44. Narrows.
45. Presbyterian Church.
46. Webb's Hotel.
47. National Hotel.
48. Adelphi Hotel.
49. Staten Island.
50. Grace Church.
51. Trinity Church.
52. City Hotel.
53. Broadway.
54. Bay.
55. Bellow's Island.
56. Ellis's Island.
57. Franklin Hall.
58. Jersey City.
59. Hoboken.
60. Emmett's Monument.
61. St. Paul's.
62. General Montgomery's Monument.

ANONYMOUS

A Description of a View of New York, Now Exhibiting at the Panorama, Leicester Square, ca. 1836
Colored wood engraving
Eno Collection, Miriam and Ira D. Wallach Division of Art, Prints and Photographs, New York Public Library,
Astor, Lenox, and Tilden Foundations

Before the existence of photography—and long before there were IMAX theaters and photo-stitching apps—a British artist named Robert Barker developed realistic, 360-degree images called panoramas. Barker coined the name from the Greek words pan ("all") and horama ("view") to describe his circular paintings, immense in size and highly technical in perspective. In 1793, at Leicester Square in London, Barker opened an architectural oddity called the Panorama, a double-rotunda gallery with cylindrical walls 820 feet in circumference, offering grand, surround-sight experiences of countrysides, cityscapes, and battle scenes. The admission price gave patrons (up to 350 at a time) a fifteen- or twenty-minute-long immersive viewing session—sometimes with an orientation pamphlet such as the one above, which depicts the junction of Chambers Street (now Park Row) and Broadway in downtown Manhattan. The scene is eerily devoid of people; the Panorama's visitors became the panorama's inhabitants.

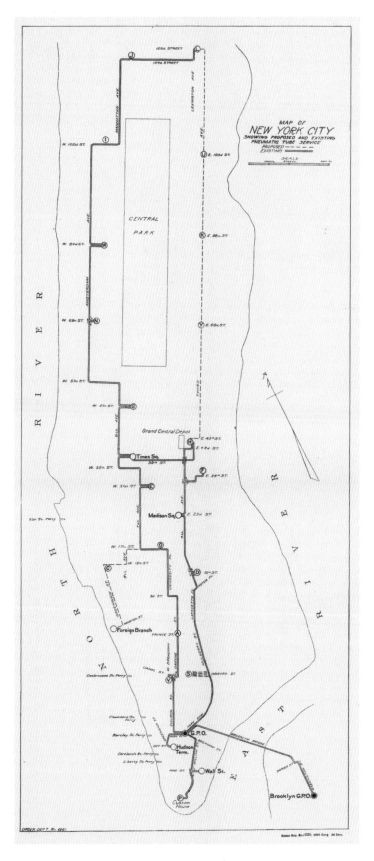

*Map of New York City
Showing Proposed and Existing
Pneumatic Tube Service,* 1908
Congressional document
17 x 7½ in.

With the advent of telegraphy in the 1850s, people became accustomed to receiving fast communications. But when telegrams became generally affordable, their popularity slowed down delivery times. Whoosh! In came pneumatic tubes to save the day (and, for a while longer, handwriting). Beginning in 1897, a system of tubing carried letters and documents up and down Manhattan, powered by compressed air from giant steam engines. It took roughly sixteen minutes for a missive to travel from the General Post Office at Herald Square either north to the Manhattanville station or south to the Brooklyn GPO.

The invention of the truck in 1912 eventually brought about the demise of New York's network; the last canister crossed the Brooklyn Bridge in 1953. Yet pneumatic magic in New York is not gone: on Roosevelt Island, to this day, giant AVAC systems suck away household garbage. Steampunk lives.

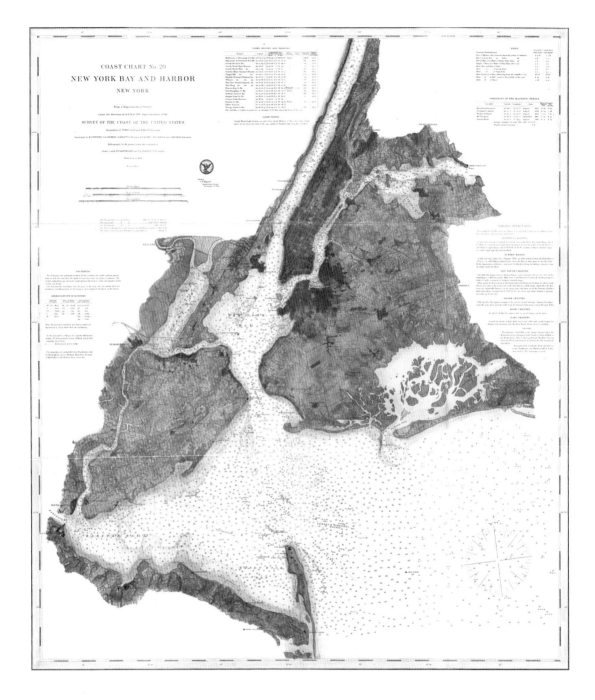

UNITED STATES COAST SURVEY

Coast Chart No. 20: New York Bay and Harbor, 1866
Hand-colored lithograph
Courtesy Geographicus Rare Antique Maps
via Wikimedia Commons

This highly detailed nautical chart includes information on lighthouses, beacons, tides, and magnetic variations. Directions to sailors are generously given; for example, "the Currents of half Ebb, in the Swash Channel, are to the Eastward strong; strangers must beware of being drifted on the Romer shoal." Duly noted.

3 SYMPATHETIC, ABSORBENT STATES VOLUNTEER TO SERVE AS NYC STORM SURGE BUFFERS

MICHAEL CRAWFORD

Three Sympathetic, Absorbent States Volunteer to Serve as NYC Storm Surge Buffers, 2012
Ink and watercolor on board
22 x 30 in.

A kind gesture. It's simply a matter of getting them to us in time.

FOLLOWING PAGE

SIMONETTA MORO

From the series, *Crossing Prospect Expressway,* 2015 (detail)
Drawing 2 of 5
Ink, pastel, graphite, and mixed media on Mylar
24 x 36 in.

For the 2015 exhibition "Mapping Brooklyn," Simonetta Moro explored in a series of drawings the six-lane freeway that is a defining feature of her Brooklyn neighborhood. The artist drew underlayers based on maps of the 1920s and 1930s, including Sanborn atlas insurance maps, and overlaid these with images of growth and "improvement" obscuring previous city blocks and structures. Moro became an archaeological historian in reverse, building up layers of Mylar sheets representing decades of development. Here we see how some 1,200 residents of the Windsor Terrace area, whose homes were condemned, had to relocate to make way for Robert Moses's Prospect Expressway.

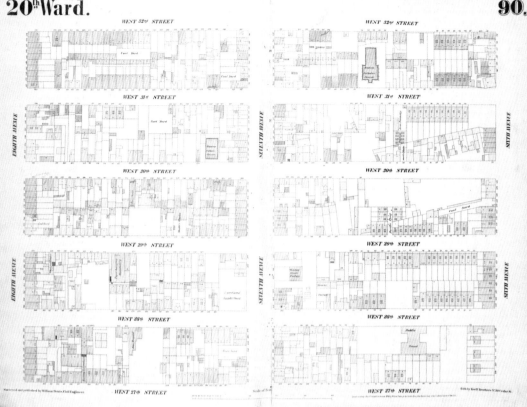

WILLIAM PERRIS

Plate 90: Map Bounded by West 32nd Street, Sixth Avenue, West 27th Street, Eighth Avenue
From *Maps of the City of New York Surveyed Under Directions of Insurance Companies of Said City,* 1852–54
Lionel Pincus and Princess Firyal Map Division, New York Public Library

On a bitterly cold day in December 1835, gas from a broken pipe ignited in a warehouse off Wall Street. The fire was fanned by gale-force winds, and in subzero temperatures firefighters drilled through river ice to access water, which froze in their hoses. By its end the Great Fire of New York had burned seventeen city blocks, razed hundreds of buildings, and caused an estimated $20 million of damage ($508 million today). Many insurance companies were ruined. Ten years later, lower Manhattan was again struck by a blaze—smaller but deadlier—that started in a whale oil and candle factory. Insurance companies again suffered.

Fire risk management became a priority for underwriters. The Jefferson Insurance Company commissioned the civil engineer and surveyor William Perris to map every building from the tip of Manhattan to 22nd Street (and, later,

beyond). Colors designated construction materials: yellow for frame dwellings, pink for brick and stone dwellings, blue for brick and stone stores. "Specially dangerous" businesses appear in green. Not surprisingly, among the most hazardous businesses (fourth out of four hazard levels) were brimstone works, tar boiling houses, and manufacturers of spirit gas, matches, and fireworks.

The cartography librarians of the New York Public Library invite you to use Perris's and other fire insurance atlases to "kill time and make history." That's the motto of the Building Inspector project, whose aim is to correlate map data with other historical documents to create a richly layered time machine. As a volunteer citizen cartographer you can check and correct building footprints, addresses, color designations, and place names. Warning: it can be addictive.

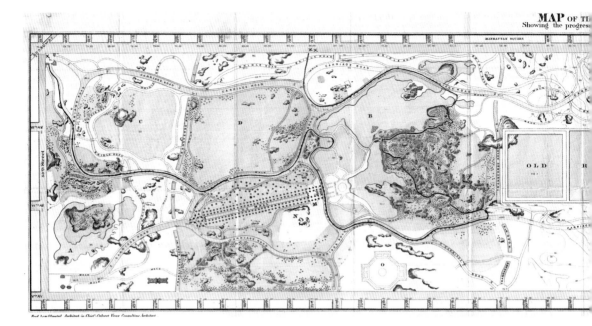

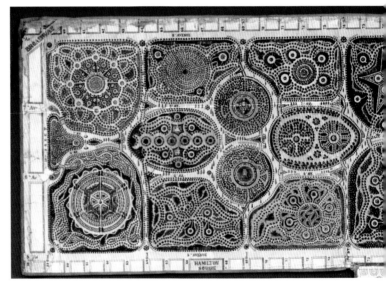

W. H. GRANT

Map of the Central Park, Showing the Progress of the Work Up to January 1st, 1860, from the *Seventh Annual Report of the Board of Commissioners for the Central Park,* 1863
Hand-colored engraving, copied from Vaux and Olmsted manuscript plan
Courtesy Geographicus Rare Antique Maps via Wikimedia Commons

JOHN RINK

Plan of the Central Park, New York: Entry No. 4 in the Competition, March 20, 1858, 1858
Ink and color washes on woven paper backed with linen
52 x 111 in.
Architects and Engineers File, neg. #81069, New-York Historical Society

Thirty-three designers submitted proposals for the design of Central Park, and in 1858, commissioners chose Frederick Law Olmsted and Calvert Vaux's Greensward Plan (at top, a map of its construction in progress). It is possible to think of the park as a remnant of Manhattan's undeveloped past, a pastoral and woodland Garden of Eden, but every bit of it was painstakingly planned. "A park is a single work of art," wrote architect-in-chief Olmsted. "Every foot of the park's surface, every tree and bush, as well as every arch, roadway and walk has been fixed where it is with a purpose." And all of this was mapped, many times.

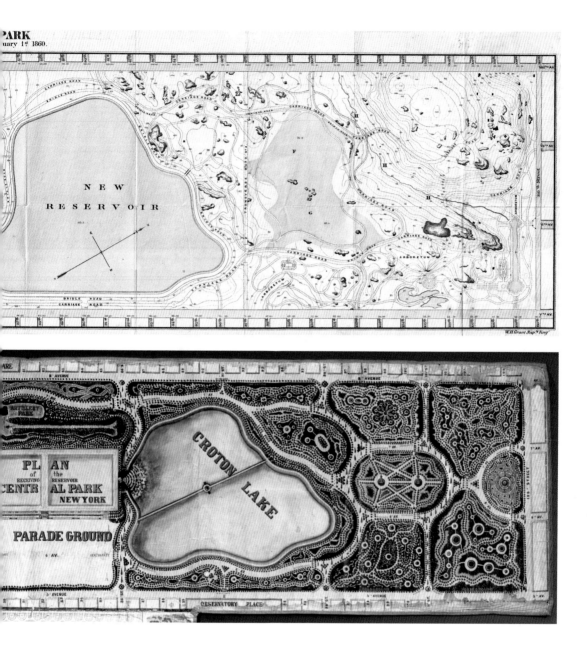

The authors of the park's Board of Commissioners annual report for 1863, which included the upper map, reported their progress in great detail. Tables enumerate vehicles, equestrians, and pedestrians entering the park; days of skating on the lakes; Saturday musical entertainments; boat passengers; and arrests in the park (e.g., forty-seven for fast driving, two for insanity). The report also contains copious construction details (6,281,670 bricks laid, 240,942 trees and shrubs installed, 7,211 cubic yards of manure used for planting) and lists of donations, which range from statuary to gondolas and animals—including, sadly, "one opossum, presented by J. Potter, Esq. (which is dead)."

This copy is marked with a black line tracing the route of the Baron of Renfrew—a title of the British heir apparent, the Prince of Wales; at that time, the nineteen-year-old Prince Albert Edward—through the park during a city visit in 1860.

Only five of the original thirty-three entries in the Central Park design competition are extant today. The lower map, from John Rink's proposal, was found in an attic more than a hundred years after its creation. It could not be more different from Olmsted and Vaux's. The topiary-driven design is so geometrically and symmetrically patterned, its map would make a lovely tablecloth.

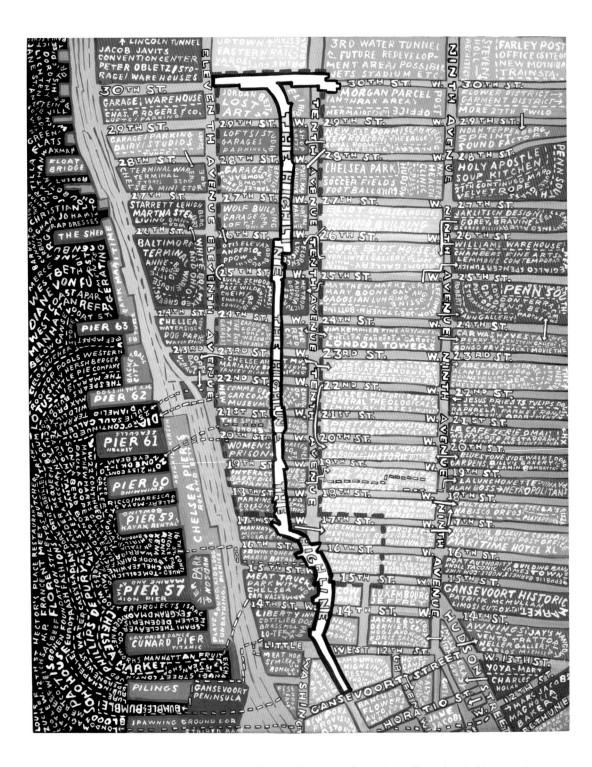

PAULA SCHER

High Line, 2005
Acrylic on canvas

Each year, five million people (and untold numbers of honeybees) visit a new city icon, the High Line: a triumphant repurposing of a disused rail line on the lower west side of Manhattan. More than seven hundred design submissions (dwarfing Central Park's thirty-three) resulted in James Corner's exquisitely planted promenade, opened in segments between 2009 and 2014. Paula Scher of Pentagram Design was involved in the effort to create the park, including designing its logo and overseeing its promotional materials. She painted this rendition for a fundraising poster.

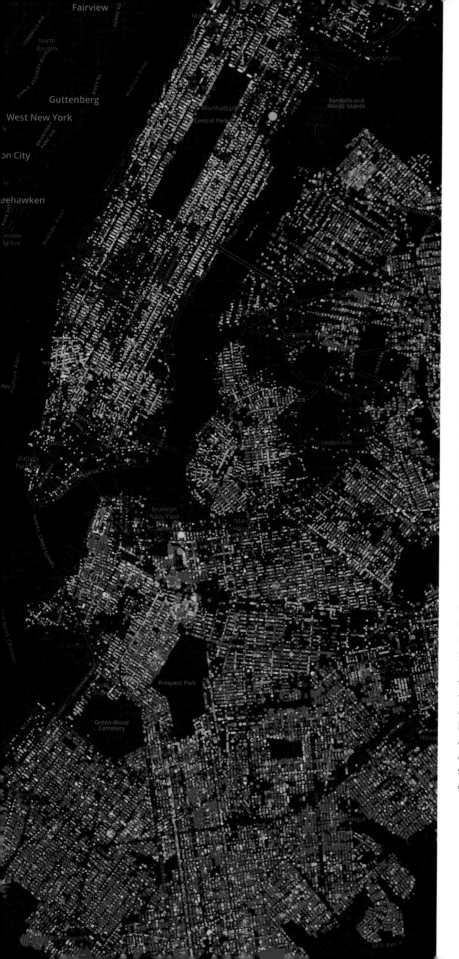

JILL HUBLEY

NYC Street Trees by Species, 2015 (detail)
CartoDB.js, SQL, CSS, HTML

Street trees comprise a quarter of the city's urban forest. Using data from the Parks and Recreation Department's 2005 Tree Census, Jill Hubley created an interactive visualization of street trees that can be filtered by any of fifty-two species; you can see all of the silver lindens, for example, or all honey locusts. Hubley was inspired to create the vibrant map while getting to know the trees near her home, whom she considers neighbors. She is partial to London planes (*Platanus acerifolia*) with their camouflage-like bark. And she's fond of a particular Eastern redbud (*Cercis canadensis*) around the corner from where she lives. "It has such nice, large, heart-shaped leaves," Hubley says, "and looks brilliant in the spring, covered with the fuchsia buds that give the tree its common name." Filter her map for the redbud and you'll see that they are uncommon—just a sprinkling of fuchsia dots across the boroughs.

ANDREW HILL with OpenStreetMap
contributors

NYCHenge, 2014
Interactive website

Native New Yorker Neil deGrasse Tyson coined the term
"Manhattanhenge" for the twice-yearly alignment of the
setting sun with Manhattan's east-west street grid. It is
an arresting sight—for the last fifteen minutes of daylight,
an orange beacon on the New Jersey horizon flares over
the Hudson and across the avenues, casting a glow
over both sides of Midtown's street canyons. DeGrasse
Tyson noted that the phenomenon's two days happen to
correspond with Memorial Day on one side of the summer
solstice, and Major League Baseball's All-Star break on
the other. He surmised that future civilizations unearthing
Manhattan "might conclude that, via the sun, the
people who called themselves Americans worshiped
War and Baseball."

Andrew Hill and team members from CartoDB, a digital
mapping tool, created an interactive visualization showing
where you can experience not just Manhattanhenge,
but also other solar alignments at locations throughout the
five boroughs, on any given day of the year. Here is
yet another thing New York offers the world: a street for
every azimuth.

RIGHT

HEIDI NEILSON

On the Ground: Breakfast Observation Area
From the Air: Winter
Selections from *Long Island City Sundial Field Guide,*
2013

Every sundial has a gnomon, the vertical element that casts
a shadow on the dial's hour lines. In the case of Heidi
Neilson's *Long Island City Sundial,* the gnomon is fifty stories
tall. The Citi Tower at One Court Square, Queens, just across
the 59th Street Bridge from Manhattan, throws a shadow
on a sundial the size of a New York neighborhood. The
lengths as well as the angles of its shadow change each day.
On February mornings, the shadow extends west across
Roosevelt Island; on September afternoons, it extends well
past the Sunnyside rail yards to the east. Take a field trip
to Murray Park between mid-April and the end of August,
and sip your coffee near the playground between
8:30 and 9 a.m. At this "breakfast observation area,"
you can watch the gnomon's shadow slide past.

Neilson has produced a field guide to the sundial, with
landmarks, maps, and seasonal walking tours. Catch the
sundial's full effect now, while you can. As Long Island
City inevitably changes, with building heights rising around
the gnomon, the New York–size calendar-clock
is disappearing.

8:14 am, April 12, Murray Park

JANUARY 1
DECEMBER 1
FEBRUARY 1

9 AM

10 AM

11 AM

NOON

1 PM

2 PM

3 PM

JANUARY 1
DECEMBER 1

FEBRUARY 1

WINTER
Shadows on the hour for the winter months.

216 E 3 St.
Block 385 Lot 11
5 story walk-up old law tenement

Owned by Harpmel Realty Inc., 608 E 11 St., NYC
Contracts signed by Harry J. Shapolsky, President('63)
                                    Martin Shapolsky, President('64)
Principal Harry J. Shapolsky(according to Real Estate
Directory of Manhattan)

Acquired 8-21-1963 from John the Baptist Foundation,
c/o The Bank of New York, 48 Wall St., NYC
for $237 600.-(also 7 other bldgs.)

$150 000.- mortgage at 6% interest, 8-19-1963, due
8-19-1968, held by The Ministers and Missionaries
Benefit Board of the American Baptist Convention,
475 Riverside Drive, NYC (also on 7 other bldgs.)

Assessed land value $25 000.-, total $75 000.- (including 212-14 E 3 St.) (1971)

228 E 3 St.
Block 385 Lot 19
24 x 105' 5 story walk-up old law tenement

Owned by Harpmel Realty Inc. 608 E 11 St. NYC
Contracts signed by Harry J. Shapolsky, President('63)
                                    Martin Shapolsky, President('64)
Acquired from John The Baptist Foundation
c/o The Bank of New York, 48 Wall St. NYC
for $237 000.- (also 5 other properties) , 8-21-1963
$150 000.- mortgage (also on 5 other properties) at 6%
interest as of 8-19-1963 due 8-19-1968
held by The Ministers and Missionaries Benefit Board of
The American Baptist Convention, 475 Riverside Dr. NYC

Assessed land value $8 000.- total $28 000.-(1971)

HANS HAACKE

Shapolsky et al. Manhattan Real Estate Holdings, A Real-Time Social System, as of May 1, 1971 (detail)
Gelatin silver print and printed and typed ink on paper
Overall: two maps (photo enlargements); black & white photographs; 142 typewritten sheets; 6 charts; one explanatory panel
Courtesy the artist and Paula Cooper Gallery, New York

For a 1971 solo exhibition at the Guggenheim Museum, the artist Hans Haacke mapped the fraudulent business dealings of real estate investor and notorious slumlord Harry Shapolsky, with maps, photos and detailed information related to 142 buildings, mostly tenements in Harlem and the Lower East Side. At the time, Shapolsky et al. Manhattan Real Estate Holdings held the biggest portfolio of properties in the city; Haacke had collected documentation connecting the dots between seventy-odd shell corporations in the group. Six weeks prior to the show's opening, the Guggenheim's director canceled it (calling the Shapolsky portion "inadequate")—possibly to avoid legal action against the museum, or due to interrelated business connections of its trustees. The show's curator was subsequently fired for his support of Haacke's work, and more than a hundred artists refused to exhibit at the Guggenheim. Ten years later, the controversial piece was included in a solo show at the New Museum of Contemporary Art, by which time it was widely known and respected.

FRANCISCA BENITEZ
Property Lines, New York, 2008
Graphite on paper, edition of 3
18 x 24 in.

The Chilean-born artist Francisca Benitez made sidewalk
rubbings of seventy-four brass plaques found around the city,
each staking claim to private property on what seem to be
public surfaces. (The markers were installed when original
building footprints changed.) Her work is a quiet response

aps can be powerful tools for urban visionaries. Planners dreaming of ambitious city makeovers turn maps of *what is* into maps of *what might be,* and suddenly, grand feats of urban re-engineering seem plausible. Take a map of New York City, for example: erase a river here, dig a canal there, bring in a lot of dirt, and—voilá! Problem solved. The map has conjured up fresh real estate worth billions.

The "problem" is Manhattan's hunger for growth. Looking at a map, a solution seems obvious: blue waterways between the island and the city's other boroughs rematerialize as tantalizing expanses of underdevelopment. Lower Manhattan, in particular—the city's birthplace, bounded on three sides by water—appears ripe with potential for growth. Through the city's history, developers have envisioned turning rivers and sea into fresh solid ground. Just add infill.

In fact, New York City began building into the water before it was New York City. In 1646, Peter Stuyvesant, governor of New Amsterdam, oversaw the first expansion of Lower Manhattan. Over the next one and a half centuries, successive expansions widened Manhattan by between one and four blocks, past Pearl Street on the eastern shorefront and Greenwich Street on the west. Old shipwrecks and garbage were commonly used to create new acreage. Today, about two hundred meters south of a BP gas station where 23rd Street meets the East River, a small patch of sand juts out from beneath the boardwalk. When the water is low, a few meters of ruins and traces of wooden infrastructure, which once supported new land, reemerge from their place in history.

In the early 1900s, the land dug up to create the Interborough Rapid Transit Company's subway line (now the 4/5/6) was used to expand Governor's Island. In 1934, the east side of Manhattan was built out on landfill and pile-supported platforms for the FDR East River Drive. And in the seventies, Battery Park City was built partially on earth excavated for the construction of the World Trade Center. But far more fantastical than the ways Manhattan has been expanded are the unrealized ways it has not.

"A Really Greater New York" was proposed by Dr. T. Kennard Thomson, an engineer and urban planner employed by the city. He suggested filling in the entire East River, thus connecting Manhattan to Brooklyn and Queens. He also proposed creating a "New Manhattan" which would have extended the island far enough south to swallow Governors Island and Liberty Island and reached toward Staten Island and New Jersey. He intended to build new islands, subway tunnels, forty miles of shipyards, dry docks, and coaling stations for massive ships. He even envisioned a new Harlem River, which would have flowed through Manhattan from Hell's Gate to the Hudson. In total, his plan would have added fifty square miles of reclaimed land to the city.

In a 1916 article in *Popular Science,* even Dr. Thomson had to admit that the plan sounded "somewhat stupendous, does it not?" Of course it did, but Thomson took heart: "Many have said 'It can't be done.' The majority of engineers, however, have acknowledged the possibility, and I have received hundreds of letters of encouragement."

With a time frame of "just a few years" and an estimated cost of the project "a great deal more than the sum involved in the construction of the Panama Canal," Dr. Thomson's

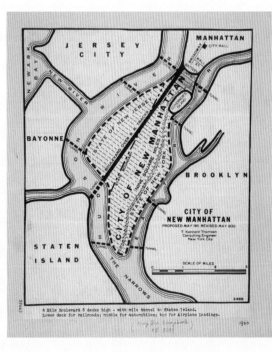

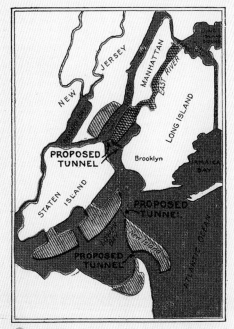

A Really Greater New York

AS PROPOSED BY
DR. T. KENNARD THOMSON.

Color indicates land to be reclaimed from the water.

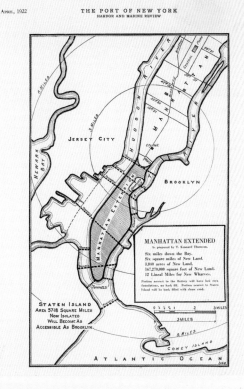

MANHATTAN EXTENDED
As proposed by T. Kennard Thomson.
Six miles down the Bay.
Six square miles of New Land.
3,840 acres of New Land.
167,270,000 square feet of New Land.
12 Lineal Miles for New Wharves.

Portion nearest to the Battery will have bed rock foundations, no back fill. Portion nearest to Staten Island will be back filled with clean sand.

STATEN ISLAND
AREA 57.18 SQUARE MILES
NOW ISOLATED
WILL BECOME AS
ACCESSIBLE AS BROOKLYN.

T. KENNARD THOMSON

OPPOSITE

City of New Manhattan, proposed May 1911, revised May 1930

Lionel Pincus and Princess Firyal Map Division, New York Public Library

ABOVE LEFT

A Really Greater New York
From *Popular Science,* August 1916

ABOVE RIGHT

Manhattan Extended
From *The Port of New York, Harbor and Marine Review,* April 1922

plans possess a charming combination of grandiosity and earnestness. While it's easy to call the project massively over-ambitious, Dr. Thomson used the reasoning of the visionary: "It is hard to realize the enormous strides of the past century, and still more difficult to comprehend the needs of the future."

In 1924, another forward-dreaming planner would propose a similarly mega-scale project. The advent of cars had brought a plague of congestion, and Dr. John Harriss, Deputy Police Commissioner of Traffic, was determined to solve it. He proposed not to fill in the East River, but rather to drain it, using dams—one near Hell's Gate at the northern end and a second near the current location of the Manhattan Bridge. Since the East River sustained heavy shipping traffic, the plan also called for a canal that would connect Long Island Sound with Jamaica Bay and the Atlantic Ocean. The land thus created would support five hundred-foot boulevards for autos and pedestrians, as well as what Harriss rightfully called an "imposing" new City Hall. Here he envisioned an expansive civic complex with music and art centers, a new theater district, schools, and playgrounds. "If carried out," commented a 1924 *Popular Science* article about the plan, "it undoubtedly will be one of the most tremendous engineering projects ever undertaken."

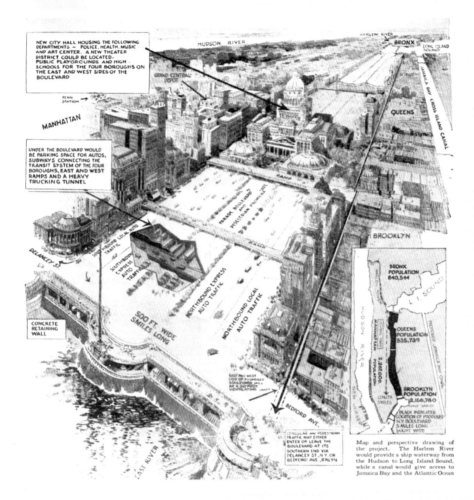

NEW CITY HALL HOUSING THE FOLLOWING DEPARTMENTS — POLICE, HEALTH, MUSIC AND ART CENTER. A NEW THEATER DISTRICT COULD BE LOCATED. PUBLIC PLAYGROUNDS AND HIGH SCHOOLS FOR THE FOUR BOROUGHS ON THE EAST AND WEST SIDES OF THE BOULEVARD

UNDER THE BOULEVARD WOULD BE PARKING SPACE FOR AUTOS, SUBWAYS CONNECTING THE TRANSIT SYSTEM OF THE FOUR BOROUGHS, EAST AND WEST RAMPS AND A HEAVY TRUCKING TUNNEL

CONCRETE RETAINING WALL

Map and perspective drawing of the project. The Harlem River would provide a ship waterway from the Hudson to Long Island Sound, while a canal would give access to Jamaica Bay and the Atlantic Ocean

JOHN HARRISS

Plan to Drain a New York River
From *Popular Science Monthly,*
December 1924

NORMAN SPER
Filling in the Hudson
From *Modern Mechanix,* March 1934

LUC WILSON and MUCHAN PARK, CENTER FOR URBAN REAL ESTATE (CURE.) AT COLUMBIA UNIVERSITY

Lower–Lower Manhattan (LoLo), 2011

Most recently, in 2011, the Center for Urban Real Estate (CURE.) at Columbia University proposed a project of similar proportions. The plan, "Lolo," or "Lower Lower Manhattan," would join Lower Manhattan with Governors Island, using millions of cubic yards of landfill. This would come from the land regularly dredged up by the Army Corps of Engineers from shipping canals. CURE. estimated that over two or three decades, LoLo would offer 88 million square feet of land for development, with an estimated $16.7 billion in revenue for the city. In a *New York Times* article, the president of the Municipal Arts Society of New York, Vin Cipolla, is quoted as saying that the plan "is unabashed about looking at the kind of things that will move regions like ours forward." But, despite its sound logical basis, the plan gained no traction.

In theory, all four schemes would have been doable. But they would have cost billions, taken decades to complete, and required political cooperation like the city has never seen. This was their downfall; despite calculations showing that such investment would more than pay off over time, the plans were quite simply too big in terms of space and time and scale. Global metropolises are composed of people whose lifespans make them disinclined to invest in the prosperity of generations to come. One day, perhaps, the maps made by city visionaries will be our 20/20 hindsight.

Ten years later, Norman Sper, publicist and engineering scholar, proposed a plan that demonstrated his promotional side as much as his engineering savvy. His vision called for pumping out the Hudson River and plugging it at both ends to marry New York to New Jersey, adding ten square miles to the city and creating what Sper called "the world's eighth wonder." The plan aimed to alleviate traffic and lack of housing which were "threatening to devour the city's civilization like a Frankenstein monster." In the canyons where the river once flowed, Sper imagined tunnels not just for subway lines but also for pedestrians and vehicles, especially heavy trucks. The tunnels would do double duty as wartime shelters; in the event of poison gas attacks, the entire population of the city could take refuge underground.

Sper saw the project's grandiosity not as an impediment but as a selling point. "If the Russians had the vision and the courage not only to build huge cities from the ground up, but to practically rebuild an empire, surely America should not be frightened at a project as big as this."

Zoe Mendelson lives in Mexico City and writes about maps, tech, love, emojis, cities, good ideas, and other semi-related topics.

GHT 1892 BY CURRIER & IVES.N.Y.

	Long Island Shore		Atlantic Ocean			Highlands of Neversink				Lower
Greenwood Cemetery			Brighton Beach			Coney Isd.	Sandy Hook		Narrows	Quarantine Tompkinsville
BROOKLYN		Manhattan Beach	Atlantic Docks	Gowanus Bay		Gravesend Bay	Fts. Lafayette & Hamilton		Fts. Wadsworth & Tompkins	Ca
			Buttermilk Channel			Red Hook Point	Bay Ridge			
EAST RIVER			Governors Isd.	Ft. Columbus			Castle William		Battery Park	Castle Garden

Bergen Point

Factoryville
STATEN ISLAND

Jersey Shore
Sailors Snug Harbor

Port Richmond
Kill von Kull

Raritan Bay

Raritan Riv
Perth Amb

of Light

NEW YORK BAY

Battery Place

Statue of Liberty
Beloes Island

Bayonne
Pamrepo   HUDSON RIVER

Centreville

Ellis Island

Staten Isd Sound
Central R.R. of N.J.   Newark Bay
Greenville

MAPPING NEW YORK CITY, ONE FOOT AT A TIME *Becky Cooper*

Manhattan's map began as we know it with a walk. In 1808, John Randel Jr., the surveyor for New York City's street commissioners, hacked his way through the forests and backyards of nineteenth-century Manhattan determined, one fifty-foot iron ruler at a time, to turn Manhattan's untamed lands into the epitome of order: a perfect grid. His quest for a straight line frequently took him into strangers' kitchens where he was unceremoniously pelted with artichokes and cabbage. New Yorkers, furious at the intrusion, often released their dogs on him. He relied on the mayor's favor to release him from arrests for trespassing. After three years, Randel unveiled his master plan: block after block that would meet at perfect right angles, and a leveling of Manhattan's hilly territory. The plan was approved and Randel and his colleagues walked again, for a decade this time, measuring and marking every intersection from First Street to 155th Street.

It is only fitting, then, that in this city, walking and mapping are particularly difficult to disentangle. (Though *New Yorker* staff writer Adam Gopnik would argue that it is precisely walking's ability to *disrupt* the grid that lends walking its particular pleasure in this town.) For every kind of walker, New York offers a different city to discover.

There's Alfred Kazin, who trips over past versions of himself as he retraces his steps in *A Walker in the City*. "I am back where I began," he explains, arriving in the Brownsville of his youth, describing a sentiment that's as psychic as it is geographic. Walking, in this book, is a way of dipping in and out of the past and of navigating mental and emotional landscapes.

MATT GREEN
Selected photo documentation from *I'm Just Walkin'*,
2010-ongoing

Santos White Community Garden

Boardwalk trash cans in hibernation

9/11 Memorial #241

Leo's Pizza

From Day 1171 (March 25th, 2015, covering a portion
of Brooklyn's Coney Island)

There's Joseph Mitchell, not at all a mapmaker in the traditional sense, who "mapped" the city by walking its streets and capturing, in prose, its most colorful characters and settings: the seductive burst of Coney Island, the carpet of sawdust at McSorley's Old Ale House. Mitchell's portraits burst so vividly with the scenes and joys of his beloved Gotham, a reader could almost navigate her way back to them.

There's Matt Green who, in 2010, set out to walk every street in New York City—all 6,163 (or so) miles of it. Five years in, he's still walking. It's his full-time job; he relies on friends and strangers for a place to stay after the day's journey. Green is an expert at seeing the micro city. Walk with him, and he'll point out the dye dots on sewage grates that indicate when an area's been sprayed for West Nile Virus. He'll pick you a handful of ripe mulberries.

Green's not the first to embark on this exhaustive approach to trying to exhaust a place: Thomas Keane traversed every street in Manhattan in 1954, and Caleb Smith completed his wandering project on Keane's 50th anniversary. Also in 2004, Columbia neurobiologist Joseph Terwilliger walked the whole of Manhattan, 1,200 miles in just ten weeks, ending up forty-five pounds lighter. He in turn inspired William Helmreich, a sociologist at CUNY, to start walking in 2008—and 120,960 city blocks and nine pairs of sneakers later, he finished walking every street of the five boroughs in 2012. Matt Green is philosophical about the endeavor. "By the time I'm finished, I'll have seen as much of New York as anyone ever has. And yet, every step I take will be deeply colored by many transient factors—the weather, the time of day, my mood, the people around me....The sum total of my experiences over these thousands of miles will be just a tiny speck, imperceptible against the immensity of this city."

But walking and mapping, even outside New York City, go together like eating and the holidays: it's hard to say which is in service of which. There are walkers who use a map to reach their destination. And there are mapmakers who use the walk—and its invitation of pure chance, delight, quirks—to discover the city of secret detours and alleys. Of the second kind, there are innumerable variants: the contemplative walker who capitalizes on the digestive rhythm of the stroll; the flâneur who subjects himself to Walt Whitmans's "profusion of teeming humanity"; the schlepper, the escaper, the rambler, the pedestrian, the wanderer.

What these amblers have in common is that walking, no matter the pace or the purpose, is the least mediated way to get to experience a place. The pavement, the elements, the strangers, the journey. The very act of walking, in fact, may create the place itself. If this is true, far from being the best way to definitively know a location, walking may be the best reminder of a space's possibility. This celebration of the infinite may be the ultimate pleasure of walking. As Matt Green writes, "Why would you ever want to know a place completely? The excitement of New York, and the whole world for that matter, is that there's always something else to see, and something else to learn, no matter how long you've been around."

✆

Becky Cooper is the author of Mapping Manhattan: A Love (and Sometimes Hate) Story in 75 Maps *(see page 143). She is currently on the editorial staff of the* New Yorker.

PREVIOUS PAGES

CHARLES R. PARSONS AND LYMAN W. ATWATER
The Port of New York: Bird's Eye View from the Battery, Looking South, ca. 1872 and ca. 1892 (detail)
Color lithograph
Each 26 x 37 in.
Prints and Photographs Division, Library of Congress

This Currier & Ives print shows the past importance of New York Harbor as a transportation hub, bristling with masts and steam funnels. A flotilla of schooners, yachts, steamships, barges, and rowboats plies the waters between Brooklyn, Manhattan, and New Jersey—the "Golden Door" through which so many Americans arrived. Pedestrians, horse-drawn trolleys, carriages, and wagons travel through Battery Park in the foreground, and trains are visible beyond.

To the right of center, "The Statue of Liberty Enlightening the World" had recently been erected on what was then called Bledsoe's Island; the celebrated gift from France was dedicated in 1886. The circular sandstone structure at center is today the Castle Clinton National Monument. Built as Fort Clinton before the War of 1812, it later became Castle Garden, an entertainment center that at various times housed a restaurant and beer garden, exhibition hall, opera house, theater, and aquarium. In 1855 it began a forty-five-year period as a processing center for more than eight million immigrants. The Emigrant Landing Depot moved to Ellis Island around the time this print was made.

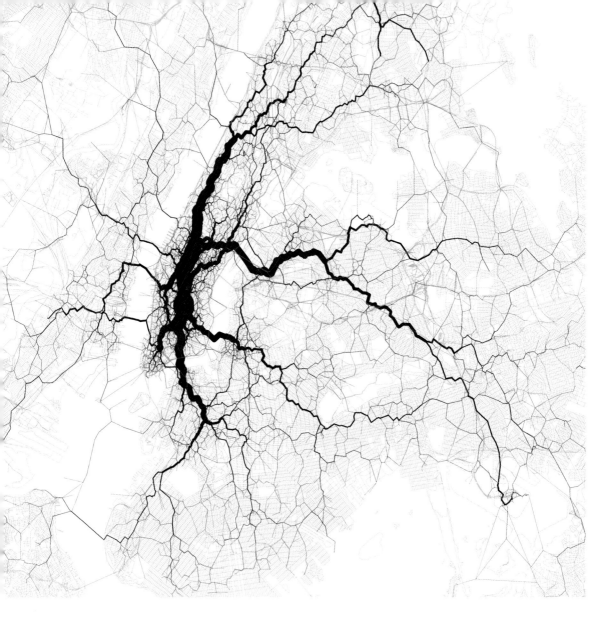

ERIC FISCHER

Paths through New York City, 2011
Data from the Twitter streaming API, August 2011
Base map data © OpenStreetMap contributors, CC-BY-SA

Eric Fischer maps the structures of cities based on the
digital data they generate. For each visualization in his *Paths
through Cities* series, he gathered ten thousand Twitter
geotags and traced routes via the densest paths of tweets.
Of this map Fischer asked: is this the structure of New York?
His answer: "Broadway as the spine is not difficult to believe."
Interestingly, the thickest lines in Lower Manhattan (including
the Broadway spine) coincide with trails made by Native
American Lenape groups five centuries ago, as illustrated in
Simonetta Moro's richly detailed map (opposite).

RIGHT

SIMONETTA MORO

*Greater New York Showing the Native American
Paths Together with the Approximate Situation
of All Known Aboriginal Stations,* 2015
Graphite, crayon, pastel, and ink on Mylar
36 x 24 in.

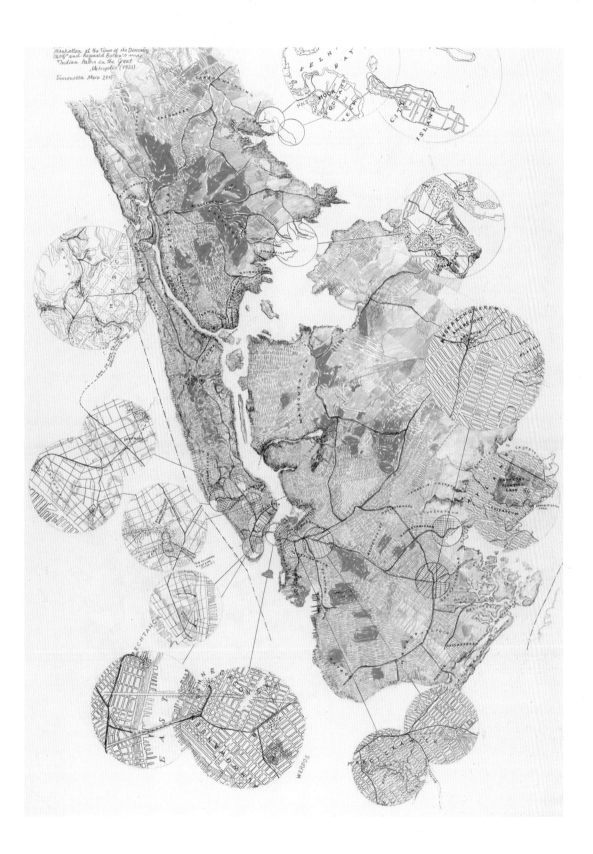

"Manhattan at the Time of its Discovery
(1609)" and Reginald Bolton's map
"Indian Paths in the Great
Metropolis (1922)

Simonetta Moro 2015

CHRIS WHONG

NYC Taxis: A Day in the Life, 2013
Digitally generated animation

Chris Whong's animated visualization allows you to follow
along as a randomly chosen taxi picks up and drops off fares
throughout the city. It's mesmerizing. You are happy for the
driver when one ride leads quickly to the next; get anxious
when he slowly trolls for many minutes at a time; applaud
his $100-plus fares; and wonder why a particular passenger
is going to Green-Wood Cemetery in the wee hours of the
night. Then, when the given medallion has clocked twenty-
four hours (shown onscreen at the rate of five cab minutes
per our real-world second), the "Load Another Taxi" button
beckons.

　　To create the project, Whong, an open-data miner and
self-designated civic hacker, requested data from the Taxi
and Limousine Commission and…well, a lengthy summary
of the months-long process he went through to produce
the site is available on his blog. Just twelve hours after taking
the visualization live, the site had eighty thousand visitors.
Its viral popularity continues.

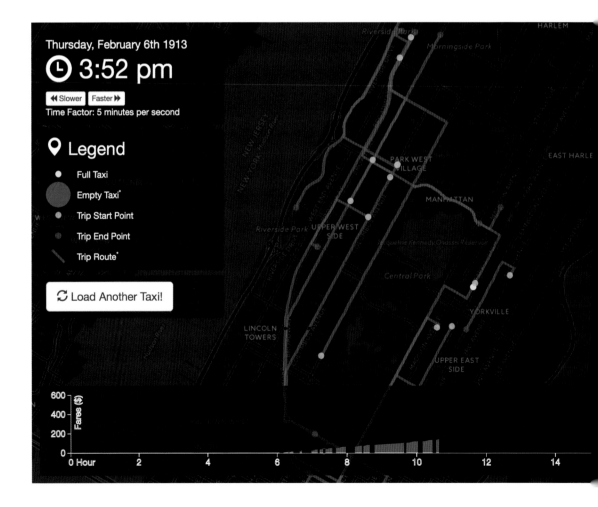

ⓒ Running Totals

Fares:	$149.00
Surcharge:	$0.50
MTA Tax:	$8.50
Tips*:	$11.40
Tolls:	$0.00
Total:	$169.40
Passengers:	17

18	20	22	24

Manhattan Pizza Delivery Routes, 2012
Still image from animated sequence in *America Revealed,*
a Lion TV LLC production for PBS and CPB

To marvel yet again at what technology has done for
mapping, watch a time-lapse sequence of a typical Friday
night in the life of a Domino's pizza delivery person. The
producers of the series *America Revealed* attached a global
positioning device to the bicycles of various deliverers, whose
shifts are depicted by blue clusters on the map opposite.

Another visualization from the segment shows the
routes by which pizza ingredients—refrigerated truckloads of
mushrooms, sausage, tomatoes, cheese—come from points
around the United States to the Domino's Connecticut supply
hub and hence to New York. A beautifully mapped chain of
deliveries ends with a steaming pie at your front door.

ENRICO MIGUEL THOMAS

Union Square Subway Commuters, 2013
Ink on New York subway map
23 x 33 in.

There came a day when the attendant at Enrico Miguel Thomas's Manhattan subway stop (215th Street) stopped supplying him with subway maps, which he uses as canvases for his depictions of various stations. Thomas then found a token clerk at 72nd Street who would hand him five maps at a time, but with a change in staffing, he was denied there, too. Now the street artist asks a friendly commuter or tourist exiting the station to get a map for him, while he stays out of sight. Every afternoon, Thomas draws at least one subway station scene, either at ground level or on platforms underground, depending on the weather. He sells his work online, and passersby sometimes purchase his works unfinished; as in his drawings, subway riders have places to go.

ASMA AHMED SHIKOH

Untitled, from the series
Home, 2010
Acrylic and ink on board
30 x 2 x 30 in.

After marrying and moving to New York, the Pakistani artist Asma Ahmed Shikoh turned her attention to Muslim reimaginings of the city. She transformed a subway map with paint and calligraphic script into an Urdu manuscript that made the city feel more like hers. "I used Urdu not only to build a personal territory within the city, but also to announce my presence and my identity," Shikoh writes on her website. "Painting the subway map and translating minute, tiresome details is therapeutic for an estranged person trying to identify with a new city, its streets, landmarks, avenues." Like a subway map, her art gave her a sense of direction. She chose to translate the map into a painting to elevate its humble status as a functional document.

DANIEL BEJAR

Images from Get Lost! (NYC), 2009–ongoing
Site-specific intervention, photographic documentation

There's something eerie about Daniel Bejar's NYC subway map—so deeply familiar and, simultaneously, strange. That's just the disjunction he would like you to feel, should you be fortunate enough to come upon it in the subway one day, and realize that the map's informative overlay is missing. In his ongoing *Get Lost!* project, Bejar, an interdisciplinary artist, periodically creates stealth installations of an altered MTA map in subway stations and cars, or replaces contemporary locations on subway signage with Native American and Dutch names. By bringing to the foreground Mannahatta's original shorelines, forests, streams, and lakes, and evoking bygone place names, Bejar draws attention to four centuries of accumulated colonial history.

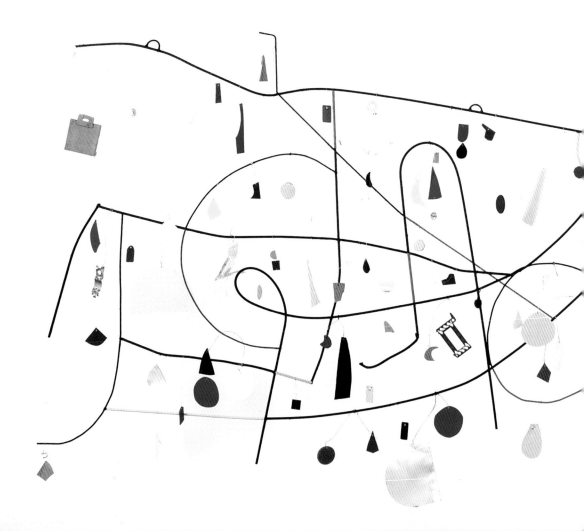
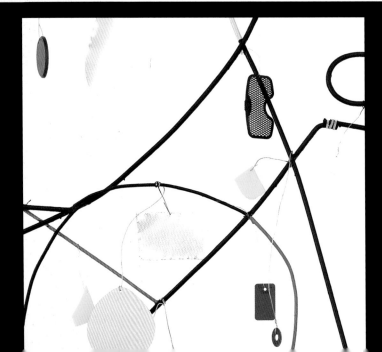

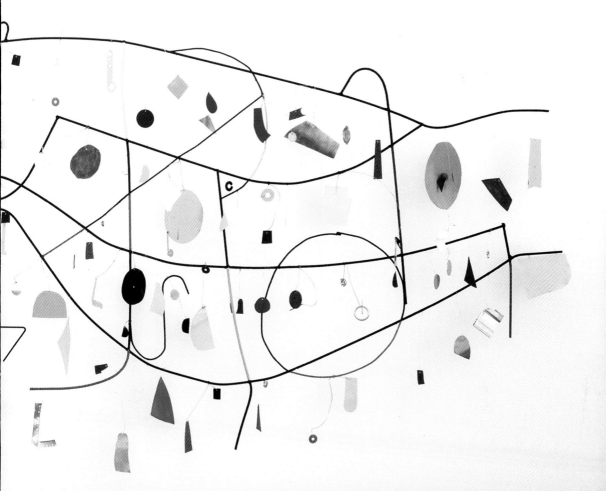

NATHAN CARTER

*BROOKLYN STREET TREASURES ALL CITY MTA
MASTER-KEY HYPING NEWKIRK AVE. TO MYRTLE
WILLOUGHBY,* 2011
Steel, enamel and acrylic paint, stainless steel wire,
Plexiglas, found objects
79 x 208 x 4 in.
Photo by Cary Whittier
Courtesy the Nancy A. Nasher and David J. Haemisegger
Collection and Casey Kaplan, New York

Nathan Carter's sculptures—and their exuberant run-on
titles—point out mapping's futilities. Made of odds and ends
of material, including street detritus found near his Brooklyn
home, the artist's lighthearted mobiles navigate convoluted
mechanical and technological systems: infrastructures
cheerfully teetering at the edge of obsolescence before
their purpose has been established.

FOLLOWING PAGE

EMMA JOHNSON

Manhattan Transit, 2014
Dissected paper maps
26 x 19½ in.

Emma Johnson wears through many X-Acto blades to
create deconstructed, multilayered maps that convey
the city's endless interconnections. This piece, one of
a series of Manhattan-related works, combines the
nervous systems of two Michelin, two Hagstrom, and

MERIDITH MCNEAL

Brooklyn Day Dress, 2007
New York transit maps and jade glue
60 x 60 x 60 in.
Collection of Catherine de Zágon

Meridith McNeal studied vintage women's magazines to develop dress patterns for a 2007 exhibition "Keeping Room," presented in a late-nineteenth-century brick row house in Williamsburg, Brooklyn. She decorated the space as a Victorian parlor and populated it with map-constructed period dresses in women's, children's, and doll's sizes. The layering of time in her Brooklyn neighborhood appeals to McNeal. "Working gas lamps still illuminate the streets along with the pinkish-orange glow of the modern sodium streetlights," she says. "Using contemporary transit maps allowed me to mimic this layering of time—providing an anchor to the present as the work allowed viewers to feel transported into the past."

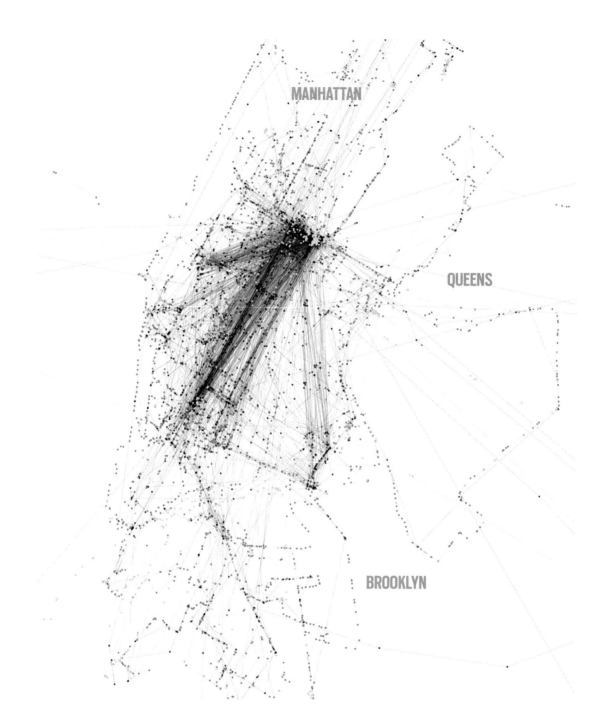

MANHATTAN

QUEENS

BROOKLYN

VINCENT MEERTENS

A Subjective Map of New York City, 2013
Digital print
27½ x 39½ in.

For the fun of it, Vincent Meertens and his girlfriend tracked all of their movements over the course of ten months in the city. OpenPaths, a personal data storing system that records locations, generated 10,760 data points—places where Meertens (shown in blue) and his girlfriend (red) spent time, with the lines between points showing routes by foot, bike, or subway. Yellow dots mark where they took photos. With visualization programming and design software, Meertens generated an image that weaves a beautiful web of daily routines and wider explorations.

AGA OUSSEINOV

The Secrets of Birds (Globe), 2012
Wood, metal, rice paper, collage, ink, gouache, and graphite
20½ x 20 x 12 in.
Courtesy the artist and TAG Fine Arts, London

Growing up along the Caspian Sea in Azerbaijan, Aga Ousseinov dreamed of vast, uncharted territories ripe for exploration. Now, as a New York artist, he is inspired by medieval European and Asian maps—diagrammatic charts that simplified routes, making arduous journeys through strange places (along trade routes, for example) seem more inviting.

The "globe" incorporates an Arabic map from the thirteenth century, when the world was thought to be two-dimensional and the flow of information was manageable (though limited or just flat-out wrong). It is juxtaposed with a map created seven hundred years later, a pre–World War II New York subway map. "I see that today's world is confused," Ousseinov says, "as it was confused when people first learned that the Earth is round." As the title suggests, those were the days when only birds knew the secrets of a map's overhead view.

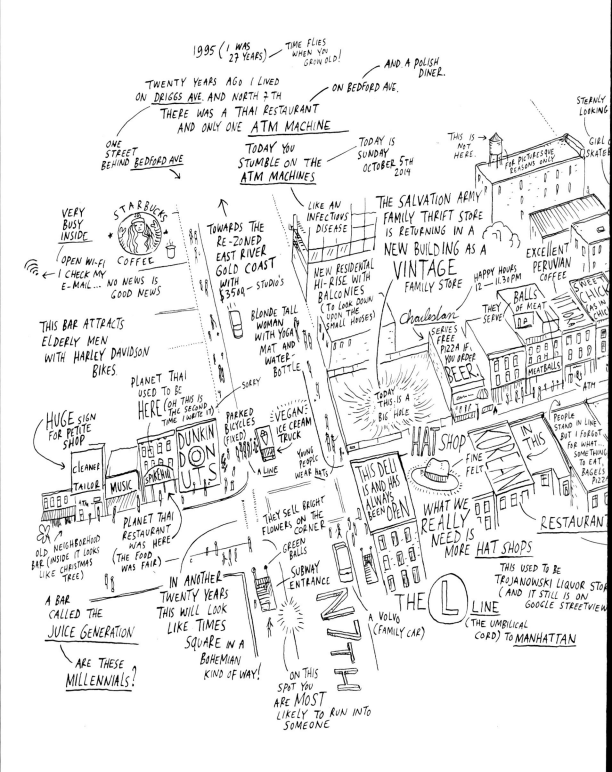

1995 (I WAS 27 YEARS) — TIME FLIES WHEN YOU GROW OLD!

TWENTY YEARS AGO I LIVED ON DRIGGS AVE. AND NORTH 7TH THERE WAS A THAI RESTAURANT AND ONLY ONE ATM MACHINE

AND A POLISH DINER.

ON BEDFORD AVE.

ONE STREET BEHIND BEDFORD AVE

TODAY YOU STUMBLE ON THE ATM MACHINES

TODAY IS SUNDAY OCTOBER 5th 2014

STERNLY LOOKING

THIS IS NOT HERE.

FOR PICTURESQUE REASONS ONLY

GIRL SKATE

VERY BUSY INSIDE

STARBUCKS COFFEE

OPEN WI-FI ← I CHECK MY E-MAIL... NO NEWS IS GOOD NEWS

TOWARDS THE RE-ZONED EAST RIVER GOLD COAST WITH $3500 — STUDIO'S

LIKE AN INFECTIOUS DISEASE

THE SALVATION ARMY FAMILY THRIFT STORE IS RETURNING IN A NEW BUILDING AS A VINTAGE FAMILY STORE

NEW RESIDENTAL HI-RISE WITH BALCONIES (TO LOOK DOWN UPON THE SMALL HOUSES)

HAPPY HOURS 12 — 11.30PM

EXCELLENT PERUVIAN COFFEE

Charleston

SERVES FREE PIZZA IF YOU ORDER BEER.

THEY SERVE!

BALLS OF MEAT

SWEET CHICK AS IN CHIC

THIS BAR ATTRACTS ELDERLY MEN WITH HARLEY DAVIDSON BIKES.

BLONDE TALL WOMAN WITH YOGA MAT AND WATER-BOTTLE

MEATBALLS

ATM

TODAY THIS IS A BIG HOLE

HUGE SIGN FOR PETITE SHOP

PLANET THAI USED TO BE HERE (OH THIS IS THE SECOND TIME I WRITE IT)

SORRY

PARKED BICYCLES (FIXED)

VEGAN ICE CREAM TRUCK

YOUNG PEOPLE WEAR HATS

HAT SHOP

FINE FELT

IN THIS

PEOPLE STAND IN LINE BUT I FORGOT FOR WHAT... SOMETHING TO EAT, BAGELS PIZZA

CLEANER TAILOR

MUSIC

SPIKEHILL

DUNKIN DONUTS

A LINE

THIS DELI IS AND HAS ALWAYS BEEN OPEN

WHAT WE REALLY NEED IS MORE HAT SHOPS

RESTAURANT

ATM

OLD NEIGHBORHOOD BAR (INSIDE IT LOOKS LIKE CHRISTMAS TREE)

PLANET THAI RESTAURANT WAS HERE (THE FOOD WAS FAIR)

THEY SELL BRIGHT FLOWERS ON THE CORNER

GREEN BALLS

SUBWAY ENTRANCE

THIS USED TO BE TROJANOWSKI LIQUOR STORE (AND IT STILL IS ON GOOGLE STREETVIEW

A BAR CALLED THE JUICE GENERATION

ARE THESE MILLENNIALS?

IN ANOTHER TWENTY YEARS THIS WILL LOOK LIKE TIMES SQUARE IN A BOHEMIAN KIND OF WAY!

ON THIS SPOT YOU ARE MOST LIKELY TO RUN INTO SOMEONE

A VOLVO (FAMILY CAR)

THE L LINE (THE UMBILICAL CORD) TO MANHATTAN

PREVIOUS PAGES

JAN ROTHUIZEN

Bedford Ave., 2015
India ink on paper
19½ x 25½ in.

Jan Rothuizen, a Dutch artist, lived near Bedford Avenue in the mid-1990s. Twenty years later he made a drawing of the area, combining his memories of it with observations of its transformation. Rothuizen creates "written maps" from wanderings through cities (New York, Guangzhou, Beirut, Cairo), talking with people and noticing details. His book *The Soft Atlas of Amsterdam* is a collection of graphic maps about his birthplace.

ALEX KALMAN
with LOLA SINREICH

Canal Street, 2010
Digitally generated image

Alex Kalman used, in his words, "the language of catalog" to map the cultural vernacular of Canal Street. The famed commercial thoroughfare—with its abundance of bootleg recordings and knockoff watches, clothes, accessories (from Louis Vuitton to Hello Kitty), and boatloads more—is a vibrant emporium of affordable delights. Even counterfeit money can be found here (but you must inquire for the price). Rolex, Rolex, getcher Rolex here.

Kalman is a cofounder of Mmuseumm, New York's smallest venue for curated exhibitions, two and a half blocks south of Canal. Its permanent collection is even more eclectic than the array in this map.

FOLLOWING PAGE

JULIE MARABELLE
New York City, 2010
Cut paper
27½ x 19½ in.

The French illustrator Julie Marabelle makes whimsical cut-paper maps of cities she loves. She begins with a series of loose sketches, joins them as one piece, and draws the entire scene on the reverse side of a sheet of thin paper. Then she uses a scalpel to cut out the negative spaces around the images and text. To see the creation of this piece—twenty hours of real-time cutting compressed into a couple of minutes, accompanied by "Rhapsody in Blue"— go to Famille Summerbelle's website. Caveat: watching the video may make your carpal tunnels ache.

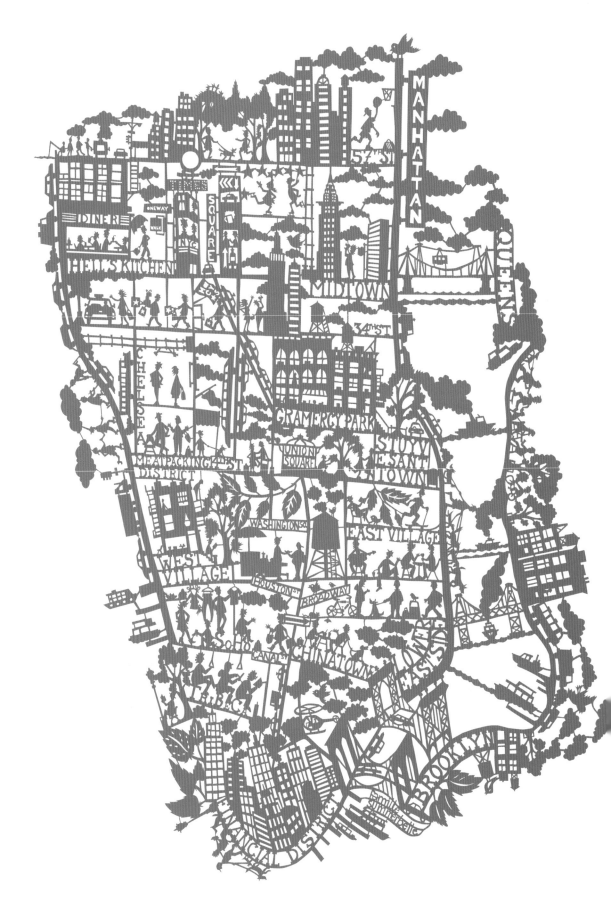

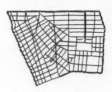

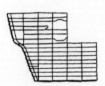

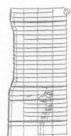

GAIL BIEDERMAN

LEFT TO RIGHT, TOP TO BOTTOM

Morningside Heights, Chinatown, Greenwich Village
Stuyvesant Town, Tribeca, Murray Hill
Chelsea, Little Italy, Clinton
From *New York City Series,* 2003
Thread on paper, edition of 3
7 x 7 in.

Gail Biederman embroidered delicate portraits of the city's neighborhoods on paper in graphite colors, to look like an urban planner's set of drafts. The disembodied shapes, like oddly devised jigsaw puzzle pieces, give character to Manhattan's divisions. "The map of Manhattan is dominated by pattern, geometry, and a strict rational grid," the artist says. "While closely based on the printed map, many of these pieces help to emphasize those moments when grids erupt and refuse to follow rules." In this case, the sum of the parts seems greater than the whole.

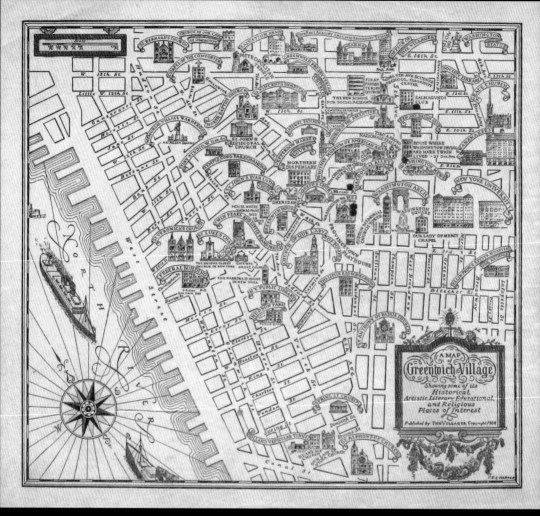

E. L. HARPER

A Map of Greenwich Village, 1934
Hand-colored map
9¼ x 10 in.
By permission of *Villager* newspaper, New York
Courtesy Old Imprints

The subtitle of this map may mislead. Though the Village
had become a cultural hub more than a century before,
the artist focuses on its churches. Aside from two dozen
religious establishments, Harper offers an assortment
of cultural attractions, including the Salmagundi Club,
the Whitney Museum of American Art, the house where
Washington Irving and Mark Twain lived (21 Fifth Avenue),
an animal hospital, and the Little Red Schoolhouse. New
York's Narrowest House (75½ Bedford Street), Twin
Peaks and the Little House (100 and 102 Bedford Street),
and Patchin Place (off 10th Street) are architectural
points of interest worth a stroll today.

RIGHT

COULTON WAUGH

Ye Symbolic Mappe of Greenwich Village, 1922
Courtesy David Rumsey Historical Map Collection

This altogether different depiction of the Village appeared
twelve years prior, in the *New York World's* magazine.
An editor introduced the map: "[The] little colony of
temperamental intellectuals has its byways and side streets,
mystifying perhaps to the everyday visitor but quite open
and inviting to the artist, Coulton Waugh, who has sought to
transcribe the passing Village life for historical records of
the future." Denizens include "a trusty Village uncle" running
a pawnshop, a fiery orator, a batik artist, a disciple of Buddha,
a poor tenant getting the boot, and a "Boobist" painter.
Eve accepts the apple and Adam grabs the snake by the tail
on either side of this bohemian Garden of Eden.

MICHAEL ALBERT

Map of Manhattan, 2009
Mixed-media collage
40 x 32 in.

Michael Albert's career as an artist has a good pun running through it. As Sir Realist, he started a juice company and used his wax oil drawings on the labels. As a self-styled "Cerealist," he began cutting and reassembling cereal boxes into Cubist pop art collages. Later he became a surreal cartographer, making exuberant if disorienting maps out of letters cut from print media and product packaging. It took him several months to assemble this Manhattan map, the first in a series. If you're lucky, you'll find Albert on the street during one of his occasional giveaways of his $50 prints; over the years, he says, he has given away thousands.

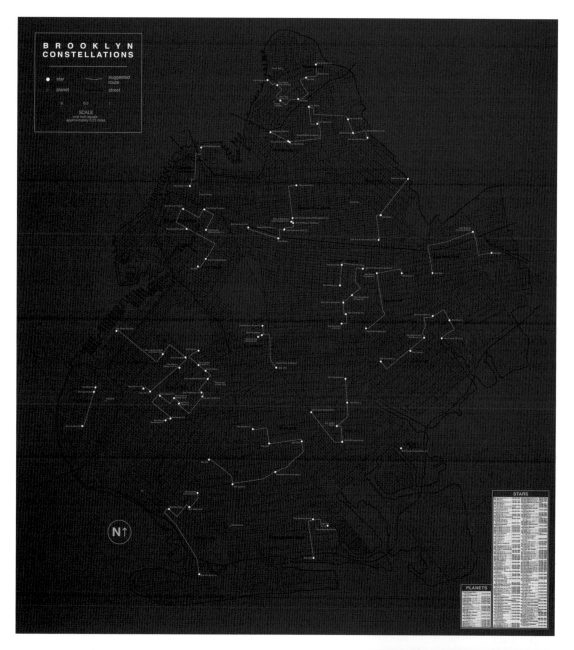

KATARINA JERINIC

Brooklyn Constellations, 2007
Digital chromogenic print, LED lights, Plexiglas, aluminum frame
50 x 45 x 4 in.

Katarina Jerinic mined the Yellow Pages to create an astronomy of a
borough. In Brooklyn's earthbound firmament, illuminated white dots are
stars, red dots are planets, and dotted lines are street routes for tracing
constellations. In Sheepshead Bay, for example, you can walk north from
Star Cuts, east to Star Sporting Goods, and then south past Planet Brooklyn
Music to Star Deli. Bed-Stuy's constellation—Star Self Service to Star Jeans
via Planet Kidz Fulton—resembles Cassiopeia or a rearing cobra, depending
on your orientation within Brooklyn's space-time continuum.

OLALEKAN JEYIFOUS

Harlem/Haarlem Contextual Empirical Diagram
From the series *Harlem/Haarlem,* 2004
Digital media on Dibond
24 x 48 in. each

Around 2000, a tide turned in Harlem: blacks were no longer the majority of residents. In his tetralogy *Harlem/Haarlem*, the Nigerian-born, Brooklyn-based artist and designer Olalekan Jeyifous explores responses to gentrification, the quest for identity, and a legendary neighborhood's continuing transformation. The work was exhibited at the Studio Museum's 2004 exhibition "HarlemWorld: Metropolis as Metaphor."

KIM BARANOWSKI
Necropolis Map: St. John Cemetery, 2010
Drawing on Xerox transfer print
25 x 16 in.

Queens is known as a borough of cemeteries. By the mid-
1800s, Manhattan was becoming severely overcrowded,
and in order to create additional space for housing, many
gravesites were exhumed and moved to new cemeteries
in rural parts of the city. Today, Queens has a deceased
population of five million, twice that of the living.

Queens cemeteries play a strong role in Kim Baranowski's
family lore. When her ancestors emigrated from Poland in
1910, they moved to Maspeth, part of the borough's
"cemetery belt," and picnicked in the local graveyards to
escape the noise and traffic of the city's streets. This
print maps the necropolis of the Roman Catholic St. John
Cemetery and charts the gravesites of Jan Ludwik Baranowski
(1843–1930) and Barbara Elizabeth Beluch (1869–

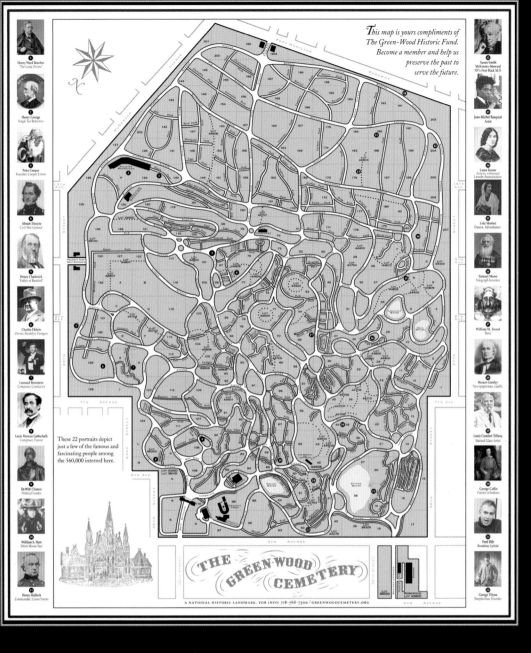

JEFF RICHMAN, JONATHAN RICHMAN, and JERRY KELLY

The Green-Wood Cemetery, 2000–2001

Color lithograph

25½ x 22 in.

Green-Wood Cemetery offers 478 acres of statuary-studded parkland for wandering and contemplation. The National Historic Monument was founded in 1838; twenty-five years later it had become a great attraction, drawing half a million visitors a year to its bucolic haven. It also became a who's-who place to be buried. Its website quotes an 1866 *New York Times* article: "It is the ambition of the New Yorker to live upon Fifth Avenue, to take his airings in the [Central] Park, and to sleep with his fathers in Green-Wood." Famous residents among the half-million people buried there include politicians, artists, musicians, entertainers, inventors, sports legends, Civil War generals, and at least two mobsters. A colony of feral parakeets nests in the spires of the entrance gates.

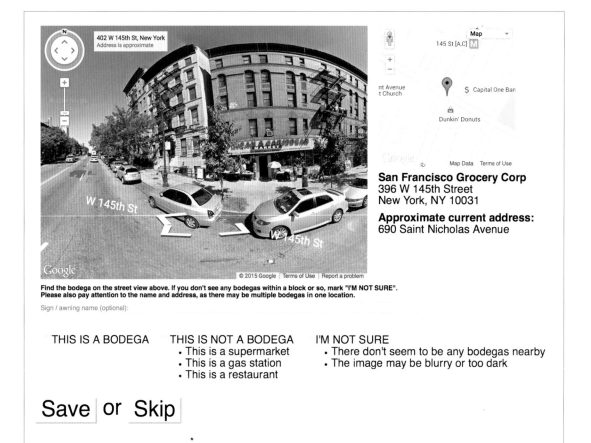

San Francisco Grocery Corp
396 W 145th Street
New York, NY 10031

Approximate current address:
690 Saint Nicholas Avenue

Find the bodega on the street view above. If you don't see any bodegas within a block or so, mark "I'M NOT SURE".
Please also pay attention to the name and address, as there may be multiple bodegas in one location.

Sign / awning name (optional):

THIS IS A BODEGA

THIS IS NOT A BODEGA
• This is a supermarket
• This is a gas station
• This is a restaurant

I'M NOT SURE
• There don't seem to be any bodegas nearby
• The image may be blurry or too dark

Save or Skip

JEFF SISSON

The Bodega List, 2010
Screen capture from site created with HTML / PHP / CSS / MYSQL

In this collaborative project, Jeff Sisson, an Internet artist, honors one of New York's most ubiquitous yet overlooked features: the bodega. These convenience shops satisfy spur-of-the-moment needs and anchor micro-communities throughout the city. Yet bodegas are so common, they can be almost invisible. In 2009 Sisson created a website where viewers around the world can place every bodega in the city's five boroughs "on the map." He compiled a list of more than a thousand bodegas from state lists of off-premises liquor licenses. Visitors to the site look at Google Street Views of randomly chosen bodegas, and use the "IS THIS A BODEGA?" tool to verify that there is, in fact, a bodega there. The definition of a bodega varies from person to person, making the project an expression of the web's collective mind and the subjectivity of mapping. Once a bodega has been verified, it appears as a red dot on the site's map. Participants thus help document a unique feature of New York's streetscapes. In the process they might consider: if bodegas disappeared, would this be a sign of progress, or provoke nostalgia—or both?

JANE HAMMOND

The Wonderfulness of Downtown, 1997
Lithograph with silkscreen and collage, edition of 45
59½ x 62 in.
Courtesy the artist and Greg Kucera Gallery

Jane Hammond reverses historic traditions in mapping
her home in lower Manhattan: the explorer is a woman, and
she is not claiming to present objective information about
conquered territory. The streets are unnamed and the grids
imprecise. Photos show everyday moments—a reliquary
for a dead bird at Tompkins Square Park, three Dominican
men outside a funeral home, a cat sitting on her front
steps—"the things the world is really made of," she says. Here
is "the wonderfulness" of creative mapping: acknowledging
subjectivity and revealing emotional responses to places
that matter to us.

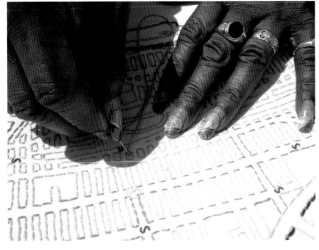

LIZ KUENEKE

Manhattan's Urban Fabric, 2010
Map, embroidery thread, cloth, and embroidery table
40 x 79 in.

From 2008 to 2013, in various cities around
the world, Liz Kueneke set up an embroidery
table with a sewn map of the city and let mappers
come to her. Passing people stopped, took
up needle and thread, and stitched locations
of personal significance: positive and negative
spaces, safe and unsafe spaces, homes and
workplaces, places where different people come
together. (They could sew embellishments of
their choice around the edges.)

In addition to Manhattan, Kueneke's project
took her to Fez, Quito, Ibiza, Bangalore, and
Barcelona. What surprised her about New York
was how forthcoming people were. "I had been
a bit scared to do the project," she says, "because
of New Yorkers' reputation for being rude and
in a hurry. But I found them to be the most open
people I encountered in all of the countries I
visited. Not only in relation to my project, but in
relation to the other people at the table—talking
and sharing with people of all walks of life."

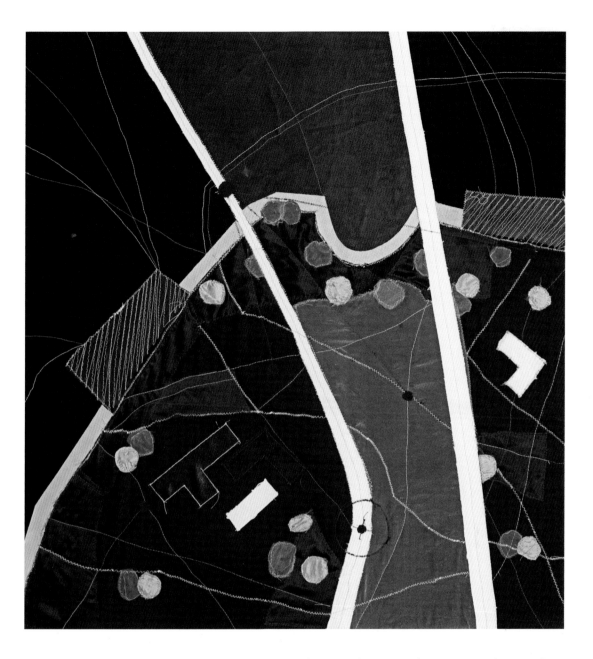

CHRISTINE GEDEON

Surrounding Dumbo, 2012
Thread, fabric, and paint
on raw canvas
32 x 30 in.

Christine Gedeon, a Syrian-born artist, created a series of large-scale works she calls "plots," part abstraction, part map. The suite draws from Google Earth and archival images, and depicts invented, utopian urban renewal projects on plots in Chelsea, Governors Island, and around the Old Stone House in Brooklyn. Gedeon says she seeks to connect "the dichotomy of the cold, analytical, masculine subject with the appropriation of traditional feminine materials, adopting a sewing machine as a mechanically precise drawing tool." Urban renewal has never looked so comfy.

CHRISTIAN SWINEHART

BDBGS!, 2010
Vector graphic displaying infestation data
from bedbugregistry.com
Map data from gis.ny.gov
Rendered with PlotDevice
14 x 9 in.

Christian Swinehart used data from
blogger Maciej Ceglowski's registry of
bedbug reports to create an interactive
visualization of reported infestations in
New York. (The maps shown here are
compilations of annual data.) Swinehart
is careful to point out that reports are
unverified, and skew toward "net-savvy"
individuals more likely to use the site.
Also, surges in reports from one year to
the next may be due to increased media
attention for the site (and for bedbugs).
But Swinehart's large map contains
wonderful anecdotal data. Click on any
dot (red for apartments, yellow for
hotels) and read tales of palpable woe.
One writer reported that an exterminator
found in a neighbor's apartment more
bedbugs than he had ever seen,
"crawling up the walls, dropping from
the ceiling—literally hundreds of them."
And the neighbor refused treatment.

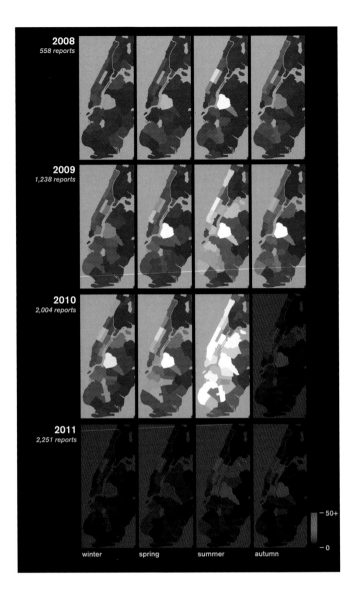

OPPOSITE

CHRISTOPHER MASON and PathoMap Team
Enterobacteriaceae Subway Map, 2015
Computer generated illustration

As its website states, the goal of the PathoMap project is to create "a molecular portrait of NYC—one swab at a time." Founder Christopher Mason's idea is to map the microbiome (all the organisms in a given location) and the metagenome (all the genetic material of those organisms) collected from city surfaces. Dr. Mason is the principal investigator of the molecular profiling initiative, based at Weill Cornell Medical College. He and his team started sampling in the subway system (from all open stations of twenty-four lines in all five boroughs), and from these specimens they identified 637 bacterial, fungal, viral, and animal species. Most of these are benign and normally present on humans. Yet the researchers found a number of disease-causing microbes, some drug resistant. And, interestingly, they discovered hundreds of species they could not identify—creatures that subway riders regularly encounter, but do not match any known organism. PathoMap data will be used as a baseline assessment of the invisible species in our midst, and repeated samplings will enable city health officials to monitor changes in pathogen populations and detect bioterrorism agents. (That's meant to make you feel safe.) Straphangers, take heart in this: of the organisms found on commonly touched subway surfaces (handrails, poles, turnstiles), viruses made up only a third of one percent.

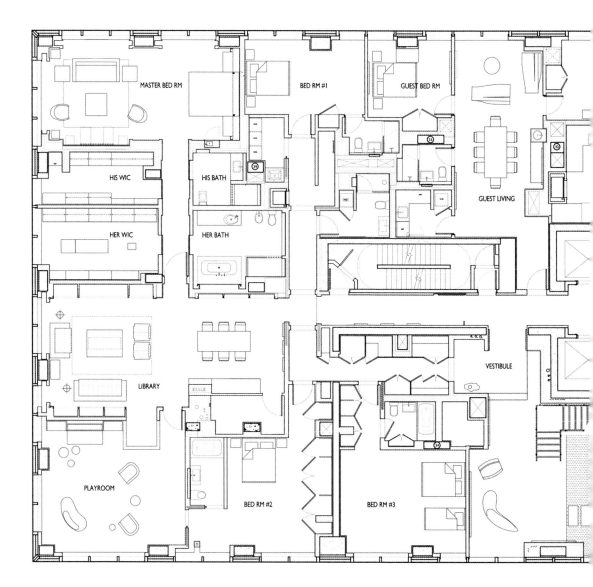

MASTER BED RM

BED RM #1

GUEST BED RM

HIS WIC

HIS BATH

GUEST LIVING

HER WIC

HER BATH

LIBRARY

VESTIBULE

PLAYROOM

BED RM #2

BED RM #3

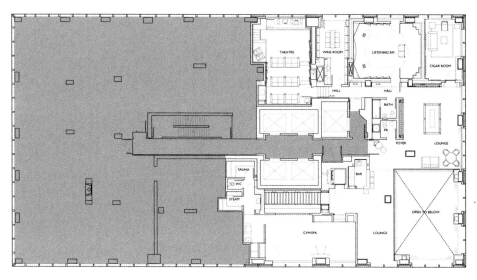

THEATRE

WINE ROOM

LISTENING RM

CIGAR ROOM

HALL

HALL

BATH

PR

FOYER

LOUNGE

SAUNA

WC

STEAM

BAR

OPEN TO BELOW

GYM/SPA

LOUNGE

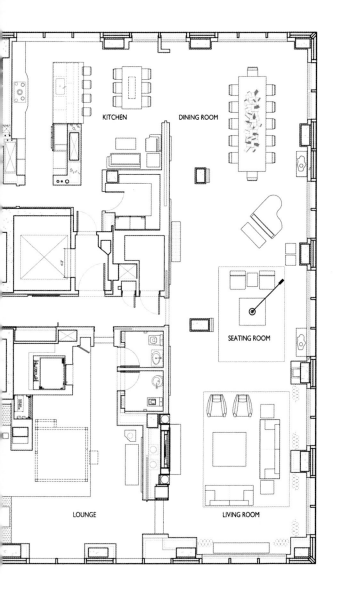

Image labels: KITCHEN, DINING ROOM, SEATING ROOM, LOUNGE, LIVING ROOM

ODA NEW YORK

Blueprints for The Penthouse, 2012

You would need to set aside a bit of time to take in the views from this duplex on the 89th and 90th floors of a skyscraper near the East River. Vistas wrap 360 degrees around the eighteen-thousand-square-foot residence, one of the largest apartments in Manhattan according to the ODA architects who designed its interiors. And you'd need these plans to find your way around. The entrance area features an indoor sculpture garden with a reflecting pool, a Japanese teahouse, and a thirty-foot water wall. On the floor above: a gym and spa, library, cigar room, theater, wine room (with racks for two thousand bottles), a billiard lounge, a bar lounge, and a listening room and recording studio. It has six bedrooms, twelve bathrooms, and the ultimate luxury: a whole lot of closets.

FOLLOWING PAGE

BERNIE ROBYNSON

In the Heart of Harlem U.S.A., 1953
Graphic poster
Beinecke Rare Book and Manuscript Library, Yale University

Lovely cupids and mermaids grace Bernie Robynson's map of Harlem, "the largest Negro community in the world." A 1936 article about the artist in the *New York Age* (located at no. 46 on the map) noted that he "finds that drawing—like any creative work—is exhausting, and for relaxation plays handball and swims at the Harlem Y.M.C.A." (no.12). This print was inscribed as a gift from Langston Hughes.

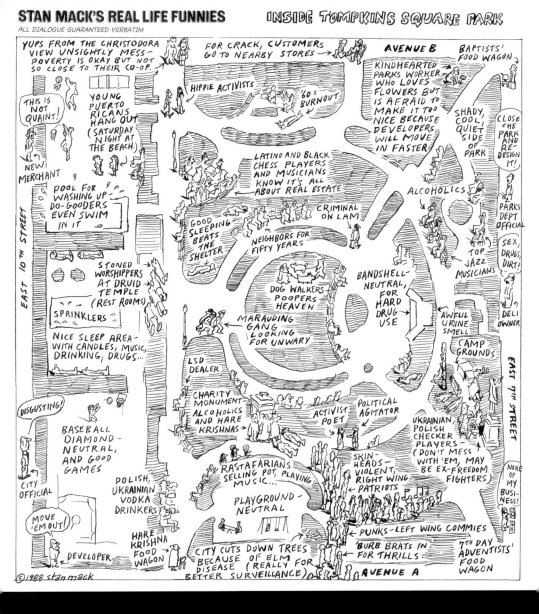

STAN MACK

Inside Tompkins Square Park, 1988
India ink on paper
4 x 13 in.

For the story of his cartoon about the East Village in the 1980s, it seems only right to quote Stan Mack verbatim. "Together, the squatters, the homeless, self-proclaimed anarchists, artists and musicians, the drug addled, and all manner of political radicals and local affordable housing activists were pushing back against the city's attempts to turn the neighborhood over to real estate interests. It was a combustible mix, full of humanity, greed, righteous anger, opportunism, politics, official blindness, and violence.

In time, the gentrifiers won, as they usually do in New York, and the East Village has become a sanitized version of its former self: decay and grunge are fashion statements, ethnic food shops advertise gluten-free-organic-locally-sourced ingredients, new glass-fronted apartment buildings incongruously shoulder their way between ancient tenement buildings, streams of NYU students and tourists flow this way and that, [and] Tompkins Park has traded live-in refrigerator boxes for strollers and kids' playground equipment."

A MAP, A TONIC, A SHOWER CURTAIN   *Sarah Boxer*

Three months after September 11, 2001, when New York was still in a deep depression, a bird's-eye map of the city's five boroughs appeared on the December 10, 2001, cover of the *New Yorker*. All of the familiar outlines were there, but something was a little off. New York had been "stan"-itized. It was as if the Middle East, with all its -bads, -hadeens, and -stans, were a veil laid over the city.

Manhattan had Mooshuhadeen, Schmattahadeen, Botoxia, and Pashmina. Brooklyn had Fattushis and Fuhgeddabouditstan. The Bronx had Yhanks and Feh. Queens, the most Balkanized of boroughs, had Irate, Irant, Hiphopabad, Bad, and Veryverybad. E-Z Pashtuns led to New Jersey. Kharkeez was somewhere in Connecticut. And Ground Zero had become Lowrentistan.

The *New York Times* sent me to investigate this wonder of cartography. I learned that the map called *New Yorkistan* began on a cocktail napkin (below). It was roughed out and watercolored by Rick Meyerowitz, who hails from Ptooey (in the Bronx), and lettered and inked by Maira Kalman, who comes from Upper Kvetchnya (also in the Bronx). Both artists, who talked to me from Artsifartsis (the Village), where they were living, had contributed the names. It began, Meyerowitz recalls, as a kind of "word ping pong."

In late November 2001, Kalman and Meyerowitz were driving out of the city to a party. The United States had just bombed Afghanistan. Meyerowitz was ranting about the tribalization of New York Democratic politics—the Sharpton faction, the Ferrer faction, like so many tribes in Afghanistan. As they passed the Bronx, Kalman blurted out: "So we're in Bronxistan?!" And the puns kept flowing: Sharptoonistan, Ferreristan. "By the time we reached the front door," Meyerowitz said, "we had forty names." The next day, a hundred: Mooshuhadeen (Chinatown), Gaymenistan (West Village), Lubavistan (where the Lubavitchers live), Taxistan (La Guardia airport).

New Yorkistan, though shockingly silly, had a serious soul. As Kalman explained in 2015, "Everybody comes to New York to escape their families, but they end up joining new tribes here. The sense of belonging, of saying 'I am connected to this tribe,' is so important." And so New York is a sweet mishmash. Afghanistan may have its tribes—the Pashtuns, the Tajiks, the Uzbeks—but, as Meyerowitz put it, "We're New York, the most tribal people on earth!"

Back in 2001, you might have thought that the last thing New Yorkers would have wanted was a depiction of their ruined city blanketed with funny names that sounded vaguely Middle Eastern. Wrong! When the cover hit the newsstands, a dark cloud suddenly seemed to lift. As I noted in the *Times*, "New Yorkers were mad for the map. They laughed. They shared it. They recited their favorite joke names....They checked out your cultural knowledge: Blahniks (the Upper East Side) is where everyone can afford Manolo Blahnik shoes. What? Youdontunderstandistan? You should be banished to Outer Perturbia (somewhere on Long Island)."

PAGES 124–7

**MAIRA KALMAN
and RICK MEYEROWITZ**

New Yorkistan, 2001
Preliminary sketches and finished artwork
Pen and watercolor on paper

NEW YORKISTAN

MAIRA KALMAN + Rick Meyerowitz

I knew New York would someday recover from 9/11 when I was deluged with letters scolding me for my mis-definition of a Yiddish word in the *Times* article. Isn't it wondrous strange, I thought, that only three months after 9/11 New Yorkers still care deeply whether *gribinez* means "cut-up chicken parts" or "chicken cracklins," and whether it ends with a z or an s? Some things will never change in New York: where there is Kvetchnya, there is hope. Seventh Avenue will always be Schmattahadeen (the rag district), and you can always find plenty of *alte kakers* to fix your Yiddish. Today Kalman and Meyerowitz's map strikes me as the "Je Suis Charlie" of 2001, but with what Meyerowitz calls a Perelmanesque twist.

Not long after I interviewed Kalman and Meyerowitz in 2001, the *New Yorkistan* poster came out, and then the *New Yorkistan* shower curtain. Did the artists become shower-curtain millionaires? Alas, no. "More like hundred-aires,"

Meyerowitz said. The vinyl shower curtain, which they didn't design, was not only ugly, he said, but had "a poisonous, horrible, chemical smell." They gave away their free samples. Not long after, they were at a party where they saw Lillian Ross, a *New Yorker* writer, unwrapping a New Yorkistan shower curtain she had gotten as a present from her son. Meyerowitz watched in horror, then took her and her son aside and warned them that if she used it without airing it out thoroughly she would probably die. It was bad, he told her. Veryverybad.

∾

Sarah Boxer, an arts reporter and critic at the New York Times *for many years, is the author and illustrator of* In the Floyd Archives, *a graphic novel based on Sigmund Freud's case histories. She has recently completed a comic-book version of* Hamlet *(with animals!) titled* Hamlet: Prince of Pigs.

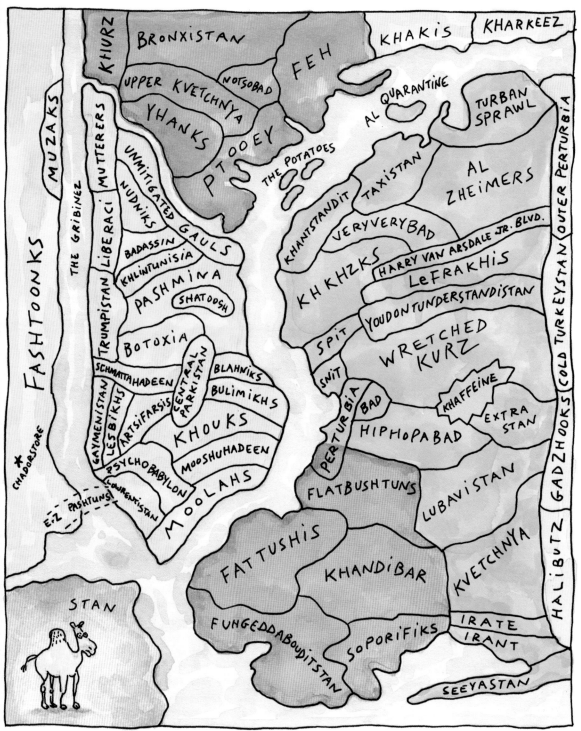

NEW YORKISTAN

5. personal geographies

FRANK	CHURCHES AND SCHOOLS	STREETS AND AVENUES	MAGAZINES
WANTABLE STRANGERS	SONGS	RIVER NAMES	STRANGERS WHO SERVE M
WHAT PEOPLE WANT	BILLBOARDS	POSTERS FOR FILMS	GRAFFITI
FEARS	HAND MADE SIGNAGE	WHAT CLOTHES SAY	MONUMENTS
TATTOOS	MOLE SKINS	SHOP WINDOWS	HEADLINES
STICKERS	ORDINARY BONES	COMPUTER WRITING	MEMORIALS
FOREIGN WORDS	MUSEUMS	RADIO TALKING	PRINTED TIPS
RACIST STATEMENTS	BULLETIN BOARDS	WORDS ON VEHICLES	PRINTED WARNINGS
AWNINGS	MEDICAL ASSISTANCE	SUFFERING STRANGERS	PRIVATE NOTES
STUFF PEOPLE SAY TO DOGS	PARKS AND SQUARES	WET CEMENT	WHAT THE LAW SAYS

MAPPING THE MARTINI *Geoff Nicholson*

When I lived in New York in the 1990s I learned to drink martinis. I often thought the Manhattan cocktail would have been more appropriate, given its name, but for me it never addressed the pleasure and pain receptors in quite the way a martini did. A martini felt more like a drug than a drink. It had my name on it. It hit hard: it wasn't for wimps.

I was two martinis to the good when I first proposed marriage to the woman who is now my wife, but who was then more or less a complete stranger. We were walking down Crosby Street, an access street parallel to lower Broadway, and I had spent a total of one hour in her company. She didn't say no.

Later, once we were an item, there were many nights when we walked through SoHo, where her office was, heading north up Thompson or Sullivan Street, and ahead of us was the illuminated Empire State Building and behind us the illuminated Twin Towers, and we said that one of these days we'd have to go up to Windows on the World, the swank bar and restaurant in the north tower, and have a martini or two. It never happened. We didn't know there was any reason to rush.

I wasn't in New York on September 11, 2001. I was three thousand miles away, in England. After the event I spent some time wondering whether I should consider myself lucky, or if I should regret having been absent at such a crucial and calamitous moment in history. There was some guilt, too, because by then I felt like a New Yorker and it seemed only right that I should have to go through what other New Yorkers had gone through.

I walked to Ground Zero several times in the ensuing years. After one of these visits, more or less five years after 9/11, I headed a little ways uptown. I needed a martini. I found myself on University Place, near Washington Square, an area where a man might reasonably find a bar to serve him what he needed. It was a busy night, everywhere was crowded, and when I saw a restaurant with a bar that opened onto the street and a couple of empty stools, I went in and sat down. I now saw that I was in an Indian fusion restaurant, not the obvious home for great cocktail making, but I tried to be positive. I asked the girl behind the bar for a martini and

a look of panic flashed across her face. This was her first day, she told me. She'd never made a martini before. She turned to one of the waitresses for help and her friend talked her through the process. For a first try it really wasn't bad.

I'd picked up a free magazine on the way in so that I'd have something to read as I drank, and now I saw there was an ad on the back page showing a map of Manhattan. I looked at it with a certain desperation. I was feeling more than ever the need to do a good, proper, constrained New York walk. I hoped that some walking route would leap up off the map and demand to be done.

Photo by Geoff Nicholson

And then—okay, I'd sunk most of a martini at that point—as I stared at the pattern of streets nearby, I quite clearly saw the shape of a martini glass. Really. A stretch of University Place formed the base of the glass. Eighth and Ninth Streets heading west formed the uprights of the stem, while Christopher Street and Greenwich Avenue diverged at equal angles to form the two sides of the conical bowl. The triangle was completed by Hudson Street, not an absolutely straight line across the top, since it contained a slight kink or rise about halfway along, but that was okay—it could be thought to resemble the meniscus of liquid that rises above the rim of a truly full martini glass.

I drew on the map, emphasizing the outline. What else was there to do but walk the streets that represented the shape of the glass, and at certain strategic points around the route find a bar and have another martini? It featured walking, martinis, exploring the city, imposing a shape on the environment. What more could a psychogeographer want?

As a route for a walk, and a bar crawl, it had its attractions. It took me past and/or into some famous watering holes: the Cedar Tavern, home of the fighting Abstract Expressionists, from which Jack Kerouac was supposedly ejected for peeing in an ashtray; the White Horse, where Bob Dylan went to hear the Clancy Brothers; the Stonewall, scene of gay resistance, though closed and available for rent when I walked by. And on Greenwich Avenue I saw, painted on a wall, the outline of a Pynchon-esque muted post horn—at least that's what it turned out to be when, the next day, I looked at the photo I'd taken of it. If you're in the right frame of mind a post horn can look a lot like a martini glass.

But you know what, all in all it was a bust. The overriding problem was that walking the streets gave no sense of following the shape of a martini glass. Even though I had it clearly enough in my head, it still didn't compute. You'd have had to be a bird or a tracking satellite or a god to see what I was doing down here.

I abandoned my own constrained walk. I walked the city feeling remarkably free, a spring in my step and several much-needed martinis in my bloodstream.

◦⟋

This piece is adapted from "A Man Walks Into a Bar,"
a chapter in The Lost Art of Walking: The History, Science,
and Literature of Pedestrianism. *Geoff Nicholson is the author*
of numerous books of fiction and nonfiction. His most recent
novel is The City Under the Skin.

PREVIOUS PAGES

SIMON EVANS
New York (detail), 2012
Mixed media on paper
37¾ x 50 in.
Courtesy James Cohan Gallery, New York and Shanghai

Simon Evans traded the familiar delineations of space in traditional maps for a floating, stream-of-consciousness grid of information that is tied less to specific locations than to ongoing observations and sensations. The key to his map includes museums and tattoos, monuments and suffering strangers, churches and schools, and stuff people say to dogs.

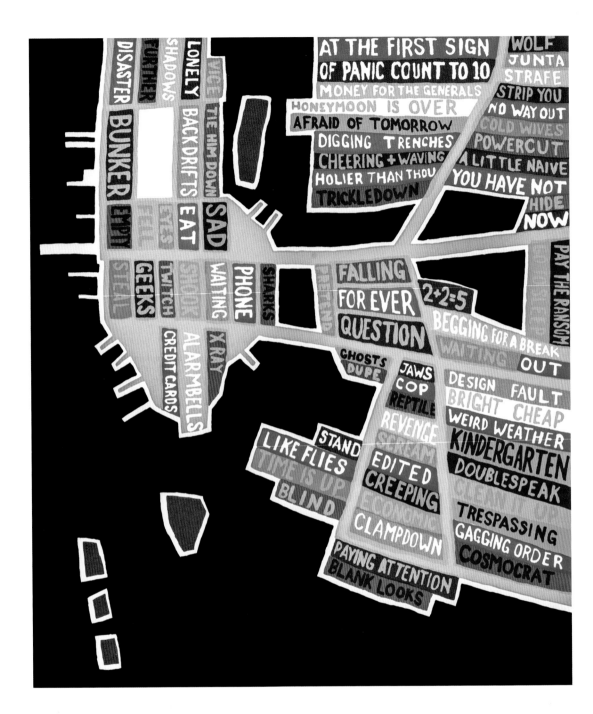

STANLEY DONWOOD

Metallic Manhattan, 2013
Silkscreen print on paper
28 x 24 in.
Courtesy TAG Fine Arts

Stanley Donwood is a British artist and author who has
been called the sixth member of Radiohead for the album
art and promotional materials he has produced for the band.
His introspective map of Manhattan, inspired by roadside
advertising, is one of several that accompanied Radiohead's
album *Hail to the Thief.*

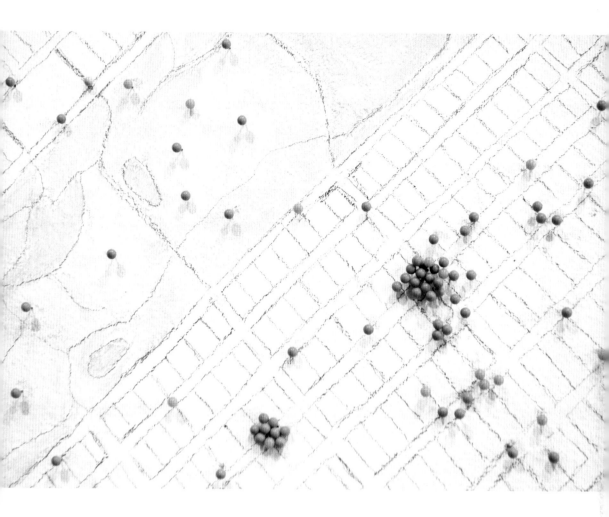

INGRID BURRINGTON

Loneliness Map, **2010**
Graphite, pastel, and pins on wall

In 2009 Ingrid Burrington started the Center for Missed Connections, a think tank devoted to the study and analysis of missed connections in various cities based on data from Craigslist. She made this map in 2010, showing missed connections in Manhattan from May through August of that year. She encourages people to think about and pay greater attention to those fleeting moments in cities that appear insignificant but linger in the memory, producing a richer and more romantic (or perhaps disheartening) experience of the urban environment.

MATTHEW PICTON

Lower Manhattan, 2011
48 x 74 in.
Newsprint, book and video covers

Matthew Picton has mapped many cities using many media. He has sculpted Dresden from a score for Richard Wagner's *The Ring of the Nibelung*, Tehran from pages of banned books, and Venice out of excerpts from Thomas Mann's *Death in Venice* and a Benjamin Britten opera score soaked in lagoon water and mud. The London-born artist, who lives in Oregon, restores to sanitized city maps the structure and grit of their histories, pointing to the forces that continually shape them. His singed map of New York incorporates headlines from newspapers dated September 12, 2001, covers from the film *The Towering Inferno*, and covers from Philip Roth's novel *The Plot Against America*.

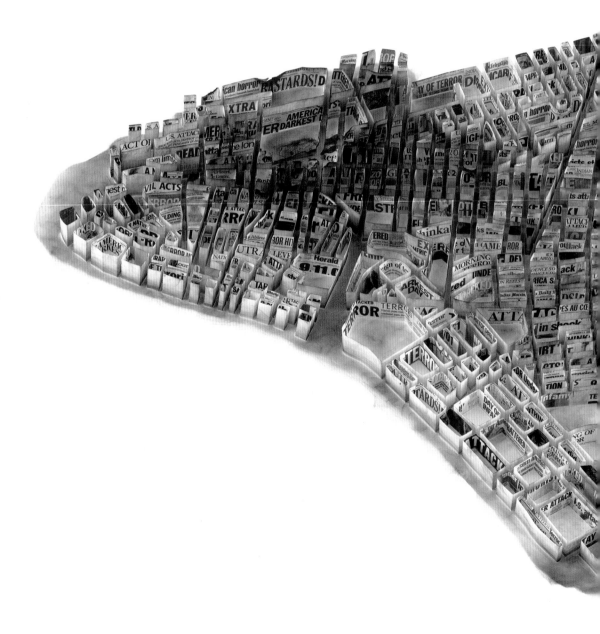

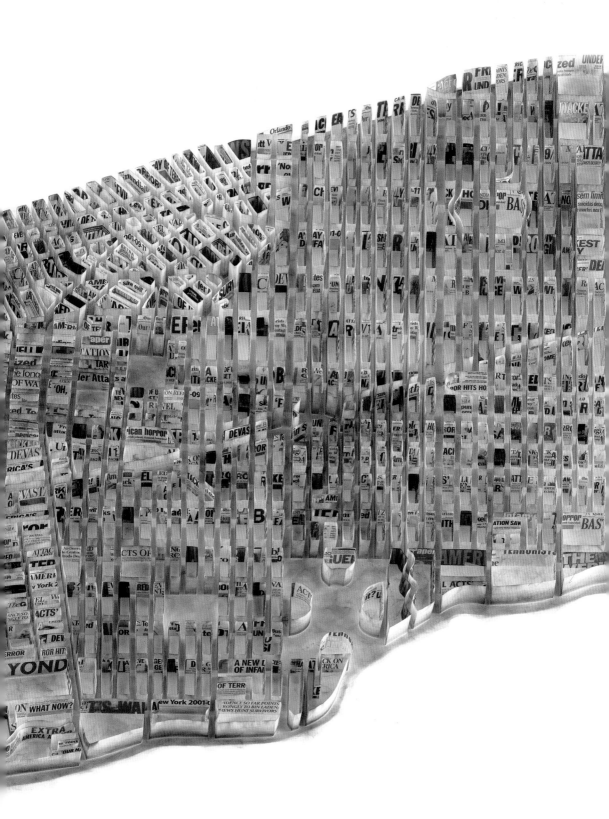

MOMO

A Tag the Width of Manhattan, 2006
Orange safety paint
Eight-mile course, two miles wide

At 3 a.m. on a late summer day, MOMO (a nom d'artiste, to protect his identity) strapped the first of three five-gallon buckets on his bike and set out to make what is undoubtedly the world's biggest work of graffiti. He traveled west to east, through the West Village, SoHo, Greenwich Village, the East Village, and Alphabet City. "Everyone was oblivious except for one guy who chased me," MOMO was quoted in a *New York Times* article as saying. "But I think he was trying to be helpful, believing I was heading to a job site and had a legitimate leak." Ironically, the scale at which the tag might be seen makes it invisible. On his website MOMO compares the size of his landscape art with Robert Smithson's Spiral Jetty, Michael Heizer's Double Negative, and James Turrell's Roden Crater. MOMO's is much, much bigger. If only street traffic, work on sidewalks and roads, and New Yorkers' millions of footsteps weren't wearing it away—but not all of it, not yet.

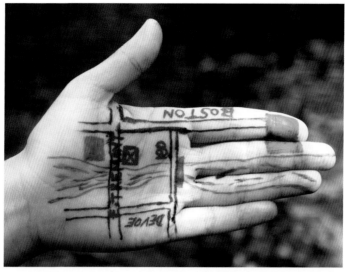

YUMI ROTH

Meta Mapa: Bronx, 2008
Photo documentation of a project
conducted for an exhibition by the Bronx
River Arts Center and Wave Hill

When Yumi Roth, a professor of sculpture
at the University of Colorado, travels to
new cities, she asks locals to draw
maps on her hands, detailing routes to
interesting places. She then photographs
and prints the hand maps to develop
a series of informal yet useful maps that
help her gain a greater understanding
of the city. During a New York trip, Roth
asked residents of the Bronx's West
Farms neighborhood to draw maps to
nearby green spaces. When she returned
with photos, an MTA employee oriented
her in the direction of a river, and a man
on a subway platform helped her get
to a park. Roth thinks of the maps as
intermediaries in interactions between
strangers, and between official and
anecdotal information. Her favorite New
York encounter, she says, "was with a
teenager, who drew a map to a hidden
chicken coop and garden in what
amounted to a median strip of land."
And she succeeded in locating it, just
under her right pinkie.

LIU JIANHUA

Regular Fragile, 2002–10
Porcelain
Dimensions variable

In 2002 Liu Jianhua, a Chinese sculptor, began experimenting with a bluish-white ceramic that is fired at high temperatures. Out of this material he created familiar household items—soap dispensers, telephones, teddy bears, boxing gloves, hot water bottles. These were displayed in a number of ways, including, at Manhattan's Arario Gallery, as a map made of hundreds of objects. A rectangle of cauliflower and cabbages forms Central Park; boots, thermoses, stacked wheels of cheese, and other vertical forms represent skyscrapers. This New York map is all hard surface and materialistic abundance, yet easily smashed.

RUTH SERGEL

Chalk, 2004–ongoing
Project documentation
Photos by Scott Jackson

Ruth Sergel undertakes projects
that combine art with history and
technology. For many years she has
conducted *Chalk,* a public intervention
that annually memorializes the 146
workers—mostly young immigrant
women and girls—who lost their lives
in the 1911 Triangle Shirtwaist Factory
fire. The tragedy instigated a reform
movement for workplace safety
regulations. Sergel located the homes
of the fire victims (most on the Lower
East Side, but others uptown and
in the Bronx and Brooklyn), and on
March 25th of each year, she assigns
the locations to volunteers who
inscribe the victims' names and ages
in front of their former residences.
The photos here, taken by the teacher
Scott Jackson, show participation by
students at Brooklyn International
High School, many of whom are
immigrants. Sergel has written a book
about the *Chalk* project titled *See
You in the Streets: Art, Action and
Remembering the Triangle Shirtwaist
Factory Fire.*

DANIELA KOSTOVA
and OLIVIA ROBINSON

Waste to Work: Anxiety Map, 2010
Mixed-media window installation
at Pratt Manhattan Gallery
5 x 7 ft.

Waste to Work: Anxiety Map was an illuminated installation,
a map of the city powered by sweat. Unemployment,
business failure, and an inability to pay bills produce anxiety;
in mapping this debilitating emotion, the artists used dots
of light to mark the locations of businesses or shops that
closed—"had their lights turned off"—during the economic
recession beginning in 2007. A variety of engraved glass jars
represented residents of the city by zip code. Using data
collected from the census bureau, Daniela Kostova and

Olivia Robinson filled each of the jars with an amount
of synthetically produced sweat proportional to the
unemployment rate in that area. The jars were turned into
galvanic battery cells lighting LEDs that represented
thousands of people on a map of the five boroughs. Marginal
areas that go from full to vacant, secure to vulnerable, are
often left out of images of the city. Sweat, the by-product
of labor and anxiety, here became a power source to draw
attention to darkness.

N.Y. MAP

statue of Liberty

(river)

empire state building

N.Y. is crowded with people!

pond

central park

Museum of modern Art

Pain quot idien (restaraunt)

taxi

bus

subway

rockefeller center

(they also have an ice-skating rink)

KEY

1. statue of liberty.

The statue of Liberty is a cool place that is a statue of a woman holding a torch, and a book. A lot of merchandise and stuff is selled there!

(Some times called Lady liberty.)

2. Museum of Modern art

The Museum of modern art has a lot of art! My favorite artist is Vincent vango.

starry night

3. Subway

The subway is one kind of transportation in N.Y. It's very dirty. And easy!

4. Empire State Building

The empire state building is one of the tallest building in N.Y! a lot of people like to go to the top.

5. Rockefeller center

Rockefeller center is crowded. I went there for christmas and saw a huge christmas tree!

6. pain quotidien (resteraunt)

this is a french resteraunt that has really good food and treats! this is the logo

OLIVIA LAPAZ
Olivia's New York, 2015
Colored pencil on paper
8½ x 11 in.

Olivia Lapaz is a nine-year-old committed artist living in Beacon, New York. From time to time she visits the city with her mother, and here she presents a guide to her favorite landmarks. The map was commissioned for this book, and as payment she requested beach glass to add to her collection.

GOWRI SAVOOR
Nyshie: Bushwick, Brooklyn, May 2010, 2010
Ink on watercolor paper
7 x 7 in.

In 2010 the Hand Drawn Map Association ran an open call for maps of New York, some to be included in a Pratt Manhattan Gallery exhibition on the psychogeography of the city. Gowri Savoor submitted one of a series of mapping portraits in which, as she puts it, "geographic features are recontextualized as body contours." Her subject is covered in a lacework of topographic lines and surrounded by the chutes and ladders of the Brooklyn-Queens Expressway, a subway station, Union Avenue, and an overreaching off-ramp of the Williamsburg Bridge. Bushwick Avenue is tucked behind her ear.

SUMMER BEDARD and contributors
I Found Your Mitten, 2010–ongoing
Project documentation

"Look down at the cold winter streets. What do you see? Lost mittens. Everywhere." So notes Summer Bedard on *I Found Your Mitten,* a website she created "as a way to turn tragedy into comedy." The California native began photographing uncoupled mittens and gloves in New York during the blizzard of 2010, mapping their locations and putting them on a website. Then she invited others to participate, via Flickr and now Instagram. Submissions come from all over the world. The photographs are poignant: a forlorn glove flattened in the middle of a crosswalk; a child's pink mitten huddling next to a car tire; a work glove, XL, caught in a storm drain; a salt-encrusted ski glove in a pile of slush. Each year Bedard anoints a mitten-finding champion. She has also thrown a holiday party for participants in her project. She can't necessarily reunite people with their lost handwear, but she can bring together those who care about them.

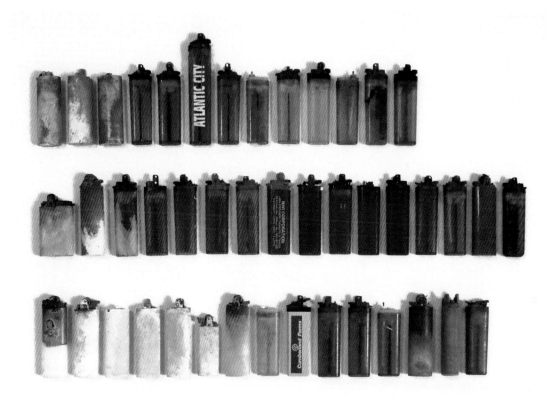

WILLIS ELKINS

NYC Lighter Log, 2011
Project documentation

Over ten months' time, Willis Elkins explored New York's terra incognita—
its walled shorelines, marshes, and rocky beaches—and searched the flotsam
he found there for disposable cigarette lighters. From forty-seven waterfront
sites throughout the five boroughs he collected 1,946 lighters, and posted
on his website photographs of his gleanings and their mapped locations.
Elkins chose lighters as his motif for three reasons: they tend to stay in one
piece, they are easy to identify, and, he says, "they seem to exist with the
right amount of frequency to keep a comber on the hunt and optimistic, but
not overwhelmed. Collecting bottle caps would make for a more daunting
experience; collecting hearing aids a lonely one." The Brooklyn artist is a true
aficionado of lighters—he knows the colors of the various brands, their design
subtleties, even characteristics of their molds. But Elkins also knows a lot
more about the city's tidal waterways than most New Yorkers. He was
not just hunting for lighters (by bike, foot, kayak, and inflatable raft), but also
for quasi-natural tidelands, unrestricted by bulkheads, among the city's six
hundred miles of shoreline.

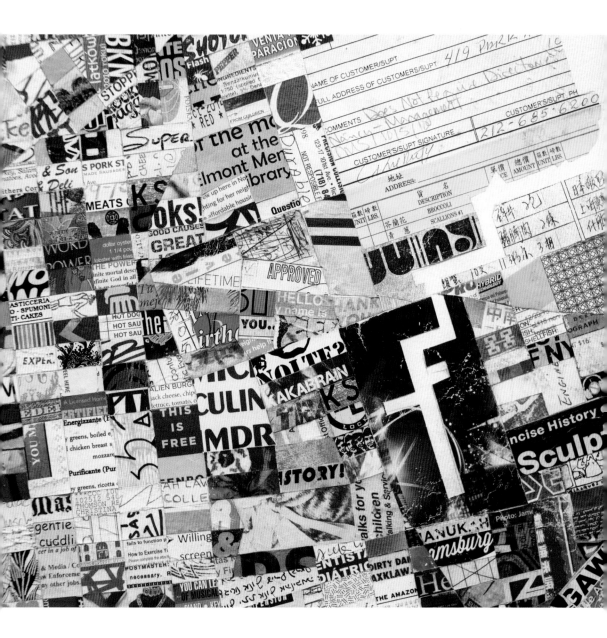

JENNIFER MARAVILLAS
71 Square Miles, 2015
Found paper on paper
120 x 120 in.

Jennifer Maravillas collected trash from every block in Brooklyn to create *71 Square Miles*, a map of the borough ten feet tall and wide. It took three years, and now she has set her sights on *232 Square Miles*. Completing the entire city will take ten years, she estimates, but in mapping the other four boroughs she is enriching the experience by inviting people to tour her around their neighborhoods. As she picks up discarded paper and other detritus, her guides give a local perspective on each accumulating block of Maravillas's giant "NYC cartograph of trash."

300 BLOCK BETWEEN EAST 18TH AND 19TH

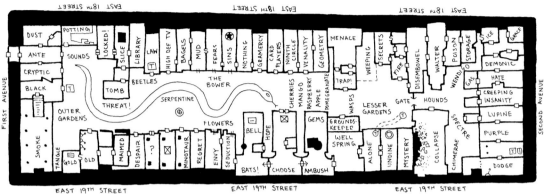

TONY DOWLER

300 Block Map, 2010

Ink on paper

4 x 5½ in.

Tony Dowler makes maps influenced by a longtime fascination with fantasy, video games, and *Dungeons & Dragons*. He believes that every map is fantastical in its own way. He tells this story about his drawing: "The *300 Block Map* depicts a particular place in New York that has a lot of personal significance, the block where I stayed during a visit to the city in 1999, with the woman who would eventually become my wife. We met when we were students, and later departed to different ends of the country: she to NYC, me to Seattle. We'd been attracted to one another, but for various reasons had never made the attraction known. We reconnected through a mutual friend via email years later. I planned a trip to New York under the cover of visiting friends, but really to visit her. Now we live in Seattle with our twelve-year-old daughter."

BECKY COOPER

Mapping: Mapping Manhattan, 2015
Pen and marker on letterpress printed card
10 x 3½ in.

During a summer internship as a college
student, while working on a map of
Manhattan's public art spaces, Becky Cooper
thought a lot about cartography—about
honesty in maps, the notion of maps as less
about geography and more as biography,
and the multiplicity of potential mappers of
the city. She embarked on a mission to solicit
maps telling personal stories of Manhattanites.
Back at school, Cooper produced hundreds
of blank maps of the island on a press
in the basement of her dorm, and self-
addressed them on the reverse side. She first
scattered the maps anonymously throughout
Manhattan, but later realized that personal
interactions—"with police officers, homeless
people, fashion models, and senior citizens
who had lived in Manhattan all their lives"—
brought her the results she was seeking:
maps of meetings and partings, lost loves
and gloves, found spouses and private picnic
spots, first apartments and near-deaths. Many
of these appeared in her book *Mapping
Manhattan,* a collection of seventy-five
personal maps, including submissions from
notable New Yorkers. Yoko Ono inscribed the
length of Manhattan with the words "Memory
Lane." Neil deGrasse Tyson illustrated the
Manhattanhenge concept (see page 68). And
Harvey Fierstein observed that although he
used to think of Manhattan as steak-shaped,
he realized from Cooper's map that it's
actually a chicken cutlet.

MAPPING THE CITY'S SMELLSCAPES *Kate McLean*

Jackson Heights, Queens: the scents of roasting corn, a timber countertop in a wine merchant's shop, curries flavored with turmeric and sweet, orange-scented coriander, plus American pharmacy interspersed with fresh-cut flowers and scorching tarmac. The hypnotic combination of these fragrances first attuned my nose to the charismatic, complex smellscape of New York.

New Yorkers are vocally vehement about the odors of their city. Every summer, news pieces decry (albeit with some pride) New York as a truly smelly place, with powerful pongs emanating from its waterways, alleyways, and street stalls. "The city's distinct smell is tolerable enough in thirty-degree weather, but jumping another sixty degrees in the summer and cranking up the steam underground is a foul recipe for disaster," wrote Camille Bautista for *Bustle*. For the *New York Times*, Victoria Henshaw wrote, "Assailed by the whiffs and stinks of Manhattan, where the gritty metallic air meets a complex bouquet of commuters' deodorant, food carts'

smoke, and festering trash, you might be forgiven for wishing your smell receptors could get a break."

It's not just the media who are repelled. Look at the comments section of any New York summer-smell-related post, and you'll learn much about the city's neighborhood odors. "The corner of Canal at Walker has a perpetual funk to it, even when the fishmonger's closed," posted one resident. Another commented, "Brooklyn summers smell like hot cat piss, Chinese food, and melting asphalt." And a third: "Trash day on 34th St at high noon on a 100-degree day—that has to be what hell smells like."

ANONYMOUS

Map Showing Location of Odor Producing Industries of New York and Brooklyn, ca. 1870
Charles Chandler Papers, Rare Book and Manuscript Library, Columbia University, New York

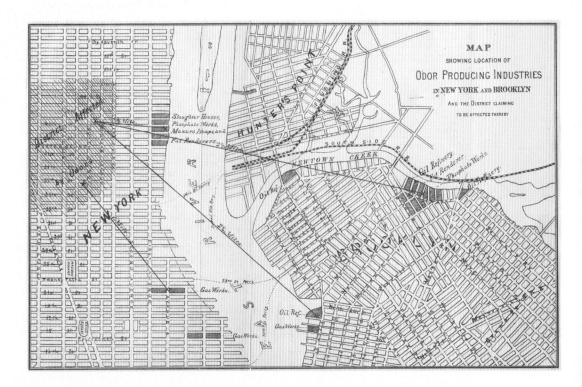

NEW YORK'S SMELLIEST BLOCKS SUMMER 2011

ELDRIDGE

DELANCEY

BROOME

STAGNANT WATER
TIMBER/SAWDUST
DRIED FISH
CABBAGE
CAR OIL
A/C

TRASH

ORANGE PEEL
5-SPICE

CHEAP PERFUME

ALLEN

©2011 Kate McLean

KATE MCLEAN
New York's Smelliest Blocks, 2011
Digital print
10 ⅛ x 6 ⅗ in.
Manchester University Library
Mapping Collection, England

In the late 1860s and 1870s, the Manhattan Board of Health actually attempted to banish smell: odor-producing industries moved off the island to Brooklyn. But smell is notoriously badly behaved; it travels on the wind. As the map on the opposite page shows, odors of phosphate, large vats of rendering fat, sulfuric acid, petroleum, and putrefied carcasses from slaughterhouses occupied a neat rectangle between 32nd and 52nd Streets, filling the area westward from 3rd Avenue. Three thin, accusatory black lines clearly indicate the smells' origins and the affected zones.

Is it possible to visualize what our noses feel? To answer that question, on a hot day in 2011, I followed a sniffing trail from the Tenement Museum to Broome Street, slowly circling the blocks (named the smelliest in the city, according to a *New York* magazine article by Molly Young) and recording every smell that drifted past my nostrils. I mapped the route's odors—of stagnant water, trash, dried fish, air conditioning, orange peel, and cheap perfume—with tinted, semi-transparent layers of scent designed to show how individual smells might move. The smell visuals occupy permeable spaces between buildings, emanating beyond the barely visible grid of the streets.

Others have mapped the city's particular perfumes. In the summer of 2010, Jason Logan took three olfactory walks through Manhattan tracing his nose's meanderings from smell to smell, embracing all equally. His encounters with dozens of fragrances included runners' sweat and Canada geese (at the north end of Central Park); shellacked church pews and wintergreen gum (Hamilton Heights); muddy shellfish, still-breathing fish, and tiny dried fish (Chinatown); and mildewy towel, metallic phone booth, and cookies mixed with

But today's smells are mere noseplay compared with the stench of the city in the nineteenth century. By all accounts, it reeked. City life entailed the proximity of hog pens, distilleries, breweries, dairies, tanneries, slaughterhouses, gasworks, and various other odor-manufacturing industries. On top of that, horse waste was everywhere. We flinch today at the odorous assault where carriage horses congregate on the corner of Fifth Avenue and Central Park South—but in the late 1800s, there were 150,000 horses in the city, producing more than 40,000 gallons of urine and three million pounds of manure per day. When it rained, the waste turned to ankle-deep sludge; when the sun shone, it turned to dust that coated every surface, outdoors and in. Street cleaners tried to keep up, carting the manure to piles on vacant lots, some of which were reported to rise higher than sixty feet. Try living down the street from *that.*

NICOLA TWILLEY
Scratch'n' Sniff New York City, 2010
Photo at left by Andreas Keller
Photo below by Nicola Twilley

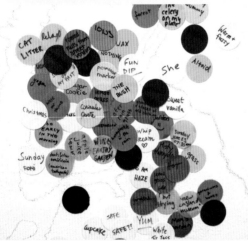

bus exhaust (Lenox Hill). With Logan we no longer find our-
selves hovering far above, in the manner of traditional mapping, but traveling nose-first, sniffing the everyday life of the
city, our toes barely touching the sidewalks. Following Logan
on his evocative tour, one can't help but smell the freshly
shaved men and freshly watered ferns, the rancid apricots
and uncooked pizza dough, or the intermingling of cigar and
Creamsicle.

Every city's subway system has a unique aroma, but only
New York has produced a crowd-sourced, interactive *Subway
Smell Map.* Gawker's mash-up (since retired) included cute
icons and odor notations such as "rat poison," "high-school
chemistry class," and "really moist, crumbly, moldy dirt."
According to the map, the subway system is a penumbra
of stinkiness. Who hasn't enjoyed, at one time or another, a

gulp of city air upon rising above the subterranean world
of the NYC MTA?

Yet human scent preferences can be highly individual. For
a 2010 exhibition at Pratt Manhattan Gallery, Nicola Twilley
created *Scratch 'N Sniff NYC* to explore not what but *how*
New Yorkers smell. Each of two maps demonstrated that a
smellscape is as much an internal, mental construct as an
external, physical reality. The first map showed demographic
differences in smell perception, based on research by Leslie
Vosshall at Rockefeller University. Vosshall and her team
asked hundreds of people from all backgrounds and parts
of the city to describe sixty-six different smells. After correlating data with DNA test results, Vosshall arrived at what she
calls "an olfactory demography of New York." New Yorkers
overall prefer the scent of vanilla, and are repulsed most
commonly by isovaleric acid ("sweaty gym socks" or "locker
room" smell). But from there, things get interesting. For
example, Queens Community District 13 (majority female,
African American, and over thirty-five) prefers the smells of
sandalwood, eugenol acetate (spicy cloves), and caproic acid
(decomposing gingko seeds). Meanwhile, in Manhattan CD
1 and 2 (majority white males under thirty-five), the pre-
ferred smells are anise, nutmeg, phenylacetaldehyde
(honey-like), and guaiacol (smoky).

Twilley also offered an interactive "personal smell favorite" map. Participants sniffed vials of scent (such as vanilla;
nutmeg; galaxolide, a synthetic musk; and octyl acetate,
synthetic orange), chose their favorite, and wrote an adjective

the bad smell | funk of 40,000 years (chlorinated) | mint | leafy green / cucumber | food / sewage | hot air soap

mint | sweet smell of childhood (burnt caramel) | coffee / glue | freshness / lushness | sweet vinegar | wheatgrass

garlic / tarmac | garlic | sidewalk spearmint | deep restful green | shattered dreams | dust

describing it—eliciting seemingly insignificant, whimsical smell perceptions. The same scent might in different nostrils evoke "cat," "6 a.m. haze," "Christmas," or "cupcake." These maps redress preoccupations of malodors in New York and engage a lived perspective, foregrounding smell over sight.

Twilley suggests that a definitive smell map of New York may not be possible. I don't think we should even attempt it! The size of the city, the subjectivity of odor perception, and the evanescence of a smellscape make the task as monumental as Jose Luis Borges's tattered map of the Empire. Instead, such a mapping could highlight the astounding, unseen possibilities of urban olfactory experiences.

What if malodorous encounters were not as commonplace? What if subtler scents produced sensory touchstones of memory? We can find pleasure in tiny instances of individually perceived smells. As industries vacate the metropolis, mass odors of factory by-products are released outside city limits, leaving small businesses to generate specialist fragrances. For example, as neighborhoods in Brooklyn become gentrified, coffee beans, wheatgrass, and beard oil suffuse spaces previously inhabited by hydrocarbons, methane, and sulfuric acid. At this micro level, the smellscape shares pleasanter offerings. In the West Village, for example, as independent stores open their doors, interior scents greet passersby. A whiff of seafood from a fish store gives way to watermelon and strawberry from a candy store, which in turn cedes to the combined scents of leather and rubber from a fetish shop. Each scent inhabits its own vortex before volatilizing into space.

KATE MCLEAN
Smell Color Sketch, Brooklyn, 2014
Digital sketch

In the summer of 2014, I organized a human-centered, experiential, emotional, expressive smellwalk around a block in Brooklyn. The resulting creative odor descriptions— "sidewalk spearmint," "the smell of shattered dreams," "hot air soap"—suggest a wider range of urban scents than the annual summer reports of BO in the subway, horse manure in Central Park, and a vegetal smell when crossing the Triborough Bridge. The resulting map (above) incorporates allusive colors and verbatim descriptions from the smellwalk participants.

The evanescent persistence and experiential qualities of small urban smells are well suited to new forms of immersive mapping. We can develop a healthy olfactory curiosity as we take our noses on walks through the city. Maybe a good time to do this is during the long winter months, when New York sits in the freezer and the more powerful smells retreat, collecting their pungency for a fresh sensory attack the following summer.

Kate McLean is an artist, designer, researcher, and university senior lecturer in graphic design at Canterbury Christ Church University, England. She is also a mapper of urban smellscapes in cities around the world.

I THINK I CAN

NORTH
(TO CANADA)

N

STATUE OF THAT GUY....

BOAT PARTIES

THE PRETTY ONE

THE TALL ONE

BROADWAY SHOWS

ART ART ART!

REAL NY'ERS
(IN A RUSH)

FARM FRESH

TOUR

FRYING PAN

TANGO SUNDAY

ROLLER DISCO

FREE

THE BEST AND THE WORST

CLASSICAL STUFF

STRAND BOOKS

PIZZA

GET HERE
GET THERE

EVERY ONE
IS DIFFERENT

BOYS IN BLUE

MIGHT SEE ANYTHING

NEW ART

OLD ART

AMERICAN ART

MIGHT BE COOL,
MIGHT BE CRAZY

ANOTHER COMMUTER

18 MILES OF BOOKS

AN AFTERNOON
EXPLORATION

LOOKING FOR
CONEY ISLAND

MY BIKE COMMUTE

A NEW YORK PICTORIAL STATE OF MIND *Antonis Antoniou*

Among the maps that keep us company, pictorial maps are invariably the most fun. They'll share wild stories, tell inappropriate jokes, even invite us for a stiff drink. And although their demeanor may seem cavalier, they are in earnest—they'll openly admit that their interpretations are embellished. New York pictorial maps are no exception; they deliver the visual goods in a New York style, using bravado and wit to praise, ridicule, or redress their own hubris. The truly special ones offer a compelling way to connect with New York's history, laugh or cringe at its absurdities, and discover surprising synchronicities.

During the 1920s and 1930s, no other kind of map better captured the zing of the Jazz Age. The pictorial maps of the Prohibition era come with a soundtrack and a cocktail, a rendition of "Zaz Zuh Zaz" with a sidecar. Entering *A Night-Club Map of Harlem* (following pages) by the cartoonist E. Simms Campbell is to be transported to that hub of revelry in 1932, with the mighty "Hi De Ho"s of Cab Calloway at the Cotton Club, the frantic dance moves, zoot suits, swanky evening wear. "Are we going in here? Yeah man!" reads one of the

conversations. Everyone wants to know, "What's the number?" (They need the line on where the hep cats is friskin' their whiskers.) Jittery lettering and wild gags energize a scene overlaid with a boozy haze. Looking at this map, I am part of the forbidden hedonism of a bygone era that today seems quaint, observing the fashions, mannerisms, and jargon of its inebriated protagonists.

In a limousine tour of the city in the mid-1930s, sightseeing becomes a thrill-seeking adventure. Al Hirschfeld's *Manhattan: A Sightseer's Somewhat Distorted View* (below) differs from the era's typically cheerful tourist maps; its depiction of the city from an out-of-towner's point of view suggests that to spend time downtown is to risk a lot of excitement. The map's capricious scales and shifting vanishing points

AL HIRSCHFELD
Manhattan: A Sightseer's Somewhat Distorted View, 1935
Ink on board
16 x 21 in.
Courtesy the Al Hirschfeld Foundation

intensify its sense of chaos. An accompanying *New York Times* article on "rubberneck lecturers" (today's tour guides) and their dramatized "spiels" explains the map's allusions, such as an odd cameo of Barnard College with a *y* to spell Barnyard ("laboriously chiseled" by a "hard-working Columbia student"), and other in-jokes.

Keeping a similar offbeat spirit but with fewer murders, Nils Hansell's *Wonders of New York* (pages 41–3) offers a merry-go-round-the-island from number 1 to 301. It's now the late 1950s and the city is a vibrant urban theater of unorthodox juxtapositions: a lobster idles by an antique armchair in Midtown, a crocodile and a mermaid hang out on Chambers Street. The loony index blends practical information and trivia, each entry a visual clue to deciphering the city. At number 32, you can "Dial ME 7-1212 for time," and at 222, find the spot where Nathan Hale was hung. Urban fauna factoids reveal that four hundred thousand pigeons live "on" the city and that "Trinity church may claim any whale caught in river." It's a snapshot of a magic hour, the gilded sides of the buildings shining with a cheerful idealism the likes of which New York would not soon see again.

Fast-forward to a decade later, and the city needs a fresh vision. Bold free-love colors advertise Norman Mailer's campaign for mayor, alongside Jimmy Breslin for city council president, in the 1969 Democratic primaries. In *New York City, the 51st State* (page 154), the duo proposes a monorail, free bicycles, and neighborhood empowerment. Pictorial maps had been used before as campaign propaganda, but conveying a serious political vision in pictorial form was a gutsy act, and somehow appropriate for these candidates. Created by Abe Gurvin, the map is a loud affair, yet its execution is relaxed. There is a festive grandiosity to the scroll and insignia, and a kind of hippie branding to the neighborhoods' logos. An airplane-morphed Capitol building delivering money directly to the city is the icing on the utopian cake. Another slogan for the map could be one of the campaign's emphatic statements: "New York Gets an Imagination—or It Dies!" Though Mailer failed to get elected, the map lives on as a kaleidoscopic relic of 1960s optimism.

While politicians may have abandoned imagination, more recent pictorial maps haven't run out of it. A fusion of humor and geography celebrates New York's triumphs, lambasts its

PREVIOUS PAGES

LEIF PARSONS
NYC for SVA, 2005
Mixed-media poster commissioned by the School of Visual Arts
28 x 44 in.

FOLLOWING PAGES

E. SIMMS CAMPBELL
A Night-Club Map of Harlem, 1933
From *Manhattan: A Weekly for Wakeful New Yorkers,*
January 18, 1933
Courtesy PBA Galleries

A "RELIEF" MAP OF GREENWICH VILLAGE IN THE FEB. 1 MANHATTAN

ABE GURVIN

*New York City, the 51st State: Mailer for Mayor,
Breslin for City Council President,* 1969
Courtesy Chisholm Larsson Gallery

In case pictorial maps needed more street cred, hip-hop giants the Wu-Tang Clan created a visual of New York to mark the group's territorial origins, *Shaolin & Environs* (page 162). The geographic mash-up presents the collective's hometown of Staten Island, or "Shaolin," with Buddhist temples marking the neighborhoods that shaped the musicians' lives and music. The style is similar to a treasure map, or a bootleg map of a lost world, giving New York the spiritual hue of a sacred metropolis. The transformation springs from the influences of Eastern martial arts and philosophy. I connect this to their own journey, the boys from the projects turned hip-hop superheroes in a city that breeds both conquerors and villains.

Jason Polan's *The Best Spots to Sit and Read a Book in Lower Manhattan* has a similarly geeky appeal (page 185). The map is a kind of personal taxonomy of urban street furniture, and an invitation to indulge in playfully monomaniacal adventures in the city. Much like New York, it gives off a neurotic vibe and a cool exuberance at the same time. Romanticized benches mingle with designer chairs and unsung industrial paraphernalia—crates, bins, buckets, cinder blocks. The Bertoias in Midtown, the High Line's peeled-up benches, the humble plastic folding chairs, all have distinctive stories to share. I imagine their day-to-day interactions with a succession of bodies in awkward postures. Pick one, open a book, sit back (or lean, or lie, or squat), and read.

Today's mini-revival of pictorial maps invites us to delight in a cornucopia of visual styles. Yet contemporary voices are not quite as spirited as during the glory days of pictorial cartography—these days we get more sheen than satire. New York calls for highly opinionated treatments. It's also time to travel beyond Manhattan, into the other, cartographically neglected boroughs. Happily, there is a limitless supply of ideas to explore, from stories of the underground to tales of the rooftops. As New York transforms for better or worse, pictorial mapmakers will keep tapping into the city's store of inspiration and frustration, and one can only hope they will deliver with aplomb. It's always a good sign when a city's maps are full of fun.

shortcomings, or heals its wounds—front and center, on magazine covers. The undeniable poster child is Saul Steinberg's *View of the World from Ninth Avenue* (page 47), his 1976 homage to New Yorkers' geographic single-mindedness, which has been continuously revered, copied, and hacked to this day. The *New Yorker* has delivered marvelous map covers through the years, some with especially prescient and timeless qualities. Mark Ulriksen's alluring portrait of the *Center of the Universe* (page 8), for the magazine's inaugural issue of the new millennium, stars the island's uptown landmarks in fancy architectural chapeaus and, downtown, their hatless twin co-stars. The skyscrapers maintain a loose geographic relationship, but shed their pungent corporate perfume for an instant of frozen suspense, floating like astral chess pieces in a cosmic still life.

I find maps most intriguing when they reimagine the city by playing out different scenarios. In Rick Meyerowitz's *The Meltropolis 2108* (page 56), an aquatic apocalypse never looked so entertaining. The map concocts a post-cataclysmic New York, a hilarious, wet dystopia with destinations such as Beloho, Brooklyn as Forest City Ratner City, and various coffee towers loading boats with the city's life-sustaining liquid. In its parodic depiction of a fractured, sodden city, the map foretold a calamity that would become reality four years later, in 2012.

Antonis Antoniou is a designer and the coeditor of A Map of the World: The World According to Illustrators and Storytellers, Visual Families: Graphic Storytelling in Design and Illustration, *and* Mind the Map: Illustrated Maps and Cartography.

PAUL SAVITT

A Sight-seers' Map of Manhattan, 1946
From *True, The Man's Magazine*
Lionel Pincus and Princess Firyal
Map Division, New York Public
Library

In 1946, according to this map, *Oklahoma, Harvey,* and *Life with Father* were established hits on Broadway. A line of Rockettes towers over the ice skaters at Rock Center, and at the Met, Brünnhilde holds forth at decibel levels loud enough to disturb the peace at the Central Library. Up north, a Yankee pitcher faces off against a Giants batter. The legend implies that New York is out on one big endless date.

Paul Savitt worked as a successful New York advertiser for twenty-five years and then, in 1973, at the age of forty-six, decided to become a full-time fine artist. His childhood heroes were Paul Gauguin and Vincent van Gogh, who, he said in an interview, "were romantic and foolhardy, just like me."

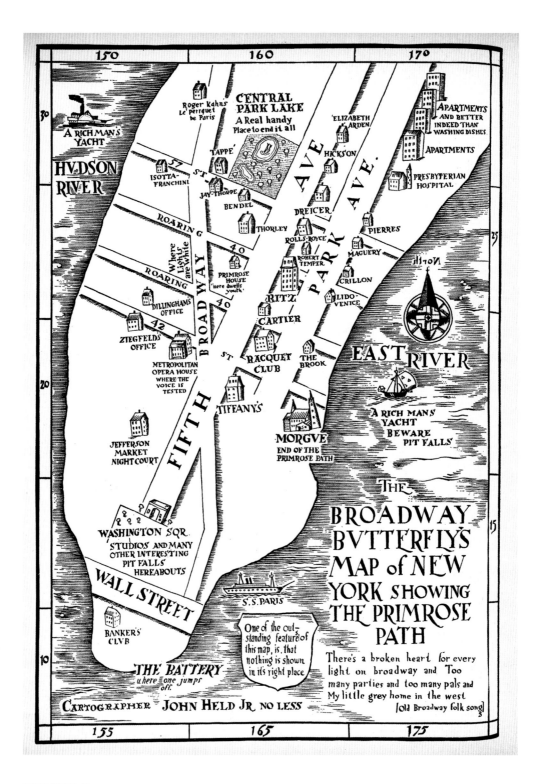

JOHN HELD JR.

The Broadway Butterfly's Map of New York Showing the Primrose Path
and *Map of New York Night Clubs, from Actual Survey by and Under the Direction of Lipstick*
From *The Works of John Held Jr.,* 1931

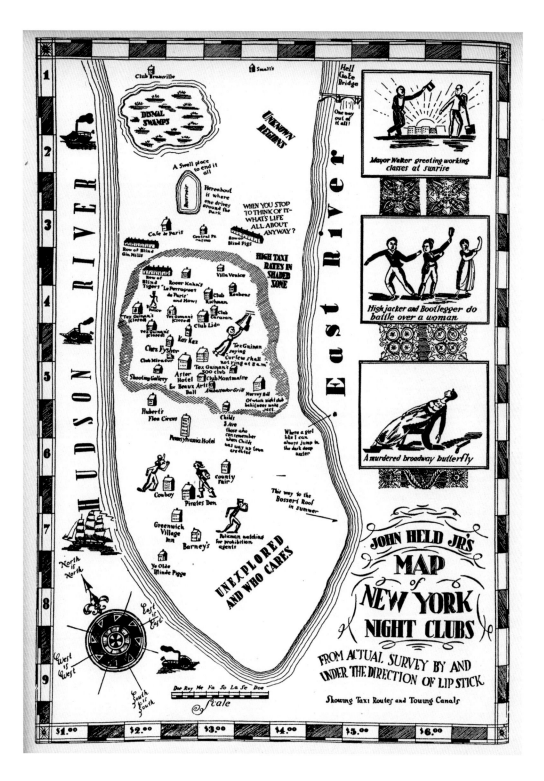

In the Roaring Twenties, "Broadway butterfly" was a sobriquet for pretty girls aspiring to become models and starlets—the first step toward acquiring a sugar daddy with jewels, furs, and savings bonds to spare. But these aspirations did not usually have happy endings. (A particularly successful butterfly, Dot King, was murdered in her bed in 1923, capturing headlines for months.) In his inimitable style, John Held Jr., renowned illustrator of the Jazz Age, depicted the pleasures and pitfalls awaiting this particular species of Lepidoptera. In both of these maps he points out swell places to end it all.

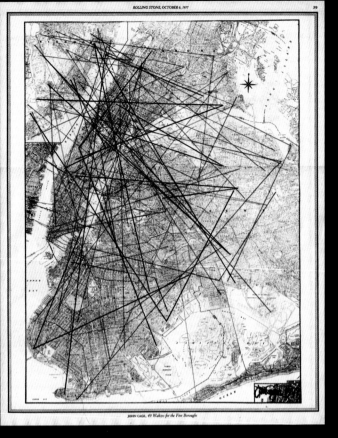

JOHN CAGE, *49 Waltzes for the Five Boroughs*

JOHN CAGE

49 Waltzes for the Five Boroughs
From *Rolling Stone*, October 6, 1977

For a special *Rolling Stone* issue commemorating its move from San Francisco to New York, the magazine commissioned a work by John Cage. He presented them with forty-nine triangles drawn on a Hagstrom map of the city. Each triangle, or "waltz," had three coordinates, equalling a total of 147 sites where anyone, anytime, could listen to the ever-changing ambient sounds of the composition. The "score" came later, when he released a list of 147 street addresses for "performer(s) or listener(s) or record maker(s)." The concept is characteristically serendipitous, with the city as performer, each participant a different audience, and a map as the structure to hang it on.

49 Waltzes for the Five Boroughs lives on in many forms. After Cage's death in 1992, a longtime colleague spent a year making video recordings at each of the sites, subsequently released on DVD. In 2012, for Cage's birth centenary, Avant Media created a website where participants can share photos and audio or video clips collected at the waltz sites. And the same year, the New York Mycological Society, of which Cage was a cofounder, presented a performance of waltzes based on recordings made wherever its members found mushrooms—a nice randomizing method.

OPPOSITE

ANONYMOUS

Gracie Emmett in Her Great Play—The Pulse of New York, 1891
40 x 23 in.
Library of Congress, Geography and Map Division

A promotional poster for a play by Howard P. Taylor, starring a vaudeville comedienne of the Gilded Age, does double duty as a perspective map showing city ferry routes and attractions. Some of the legend's points of interest (printed in red) refer to fictional locations in the play such as Mother Skevotski's Dive, Holt's Bachelor Quarters, and Dicey Moran's Haunt. Newspaper ads assured theatergoers that the play was "staged with a car-load of scenery," including a pair of trains "crossing at full speed in opposite directions." As if that weren't enough, the audience could look forward to "the Great Fire Scene showing the burning mansion and THE GREAT LEAP FOR LIFE!"

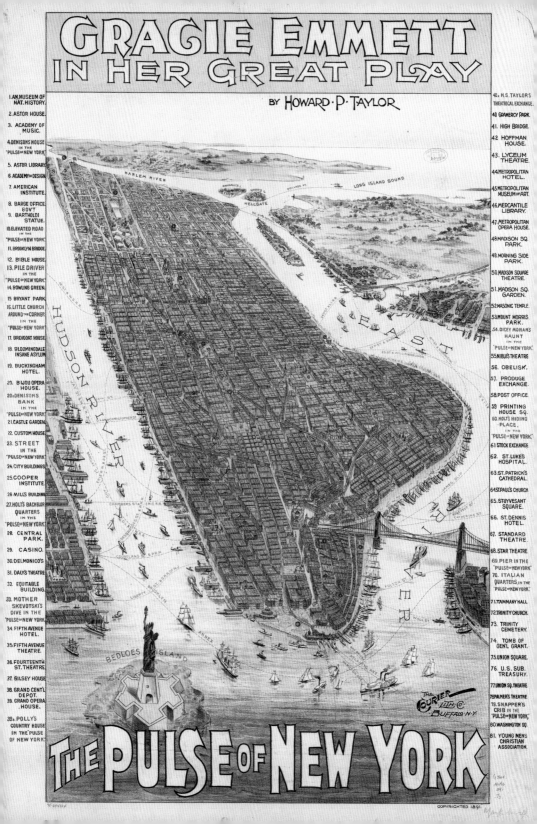

GRACIE EMMETT IN HER GREAT PLAY

BY HOWARD·P·TAYLOR

THE PULSE OF NEW YORK

1. AM. MUSEUM OF NAT. HISTORY.
2. ASTOR HOUSE.
3. ACADEMY OF MUSIC.
4. DENISONS HOUSE IN THE "PULSE OF NEW YORK"
5. ASTOR LIBRARY
6. ACADEMY OF DESIGN
7. AMERICAN INSTITUTE.
8. BARGE OFFICE.
9. BARTHOLDI STATUE.
10. ELEVATED ROAD IN THE "PULSE OF NEW YORK"
11. BROOKLYN BRIDGE.
12. BIBLE HOUSE.
13. PILE DRIVER IN THE "PULSE OF NEW YORK"
14. BOWLING GREEN.
15. BRYANT PARK
16. LITTLE CHURCH AROUND THE CORNER IN THE "PULSE OF NEW YORK"
17. BREVOORT HOUSE
18. BLOOMINGDALE INSANE ASYLUM
19. BUCKINGHAM HOTEL.
20. BIJOU OPERA HOUSE.
20½. DENISONS BANK IN THE "PULSE OF NEW YORK"
21. CASTLE GARDEN.
22. CUSTOM HOUSE
23. STREET IN THE "PULSE OF NEW YORK"
24. CITY BUILDINGS
25. COOPER INSTITUTE.
26. MILLS BUILDING
27. HOLT'S BACHELOR QUARTERS IN THE "PULSE OF NEW YORK"
28. CENTRAL PARK.
29. CASINO.
30. DELMONICO'S.
31. DALY'S THEATRE.
32. EQUITABLE BUILDING.
33. MOTHER SKEVOTSKI'S DIVE IN THE "PULSE OF NEW YORK"
34. FIFTH AVENUE HOTEL.
35. FIFTH AVENUE THEATRE.
36. FOURTEENTH ST. THEATRE.
37. GILSEY HOUSE.
38. GRAND CENT'L DEPOT.
39. GRAND OPERA HOUSE.
39½. POLLY'S COUNTRY HOUSE IN THE "PULSE OF NEW YORK"

40½. H.S. TAYLORS THEATRICAL EXCHANGE.
40. GRAMERCY PARK.
41. HIGH BRIDGE.
42. HOFFMAN HOUSE.
43. LYCEUM THEATRE.
44. METROPOLITAN HOTEL.
45. METROPOLITAN MUSEUM OF ART.
46. MERCANTILE LIBRARY.
47. METROPOLITAN OPERA HOUSE.
48. MADISON SQ. PARK.
49. MORNING SIDE PARK.
50. MADISON SQUARE THEATRE.
51. MADISON SQ. GARDEN.
52. MASONIC TEMPLE.
53. MOUNT MORRIS PARK.
54. DICEY MORANS HAUNT IN THE "PULSE OF NEW YORK"
55. NIBLO'S THEATRE.
56. OBELISK.
57. PRODUCE EXCHANGE.
58. POST OFFICE.
59. PRINTING HOUSE SQ.
60. HOLT'S HIDING PLACE IN THE "PULSE OF NEW YORK"
61. STOCK EXCHANGE
62. ST. LUKES HOSPITAL.
63. ST. PATRICK'S CATHEDRAL.
64. ST. PAUL'S CHURCH.
65. STUYVESANT SQUARE.
66. ST. DENNIS HOTEL.
67. STANDARD THEATRE.
68. STAR THEATRE.
69. PIER IN THE "PULSE OF NEW YORK"
70. ITALIAN QUARTERS IN THE "PULSE OF NEW YORK"
71. TAMMANY HALL.
72. TRINITY CHURCH.
73. TRINITY CEMETERY.
74. TOMB OF GEN'L GRANT.
75. UNION SQUARE.
76. U.S. SUB. TREASURY.
77. UNION SQ. THEATRE.
78. PALMER'S THEATRE.
79. SNAPPER'S CRIB IN THE "PULSE OF NEW YORK"
80. WASHINGTON SQ.
81. YOUNG MENS CHRISTIAN ASSOCIATION.

THE COURIER LITH. CO. BUFFALO·N·Y

COPYRIGHTED 1891.

FRANCESCA PASINI, with lyrics by Regina Spektor

Reginapolis, 2010
Silkscreen print
30 x 22 in.

Francesca Pasini, an Italian artist, spent the summer of
2010 in New York, and as she explored the city, she found
herself humming songs by the alt-pop singer-songwriter
Regina Spektor. When she returned home, Pasini created
this map of lyrics, with each handwritten "font" corresponding
to a song.

Art by TONY MILLIONAIRE, design by CINDY HO, concept by MARC H. MILLER and JOANN JONES

The Queens Jazz Trail, 1998
Offset print based on ink drawings, digitally colored
17 x 21 in.
Courtesy Flushing Town Hall

Queens, "the home of jazz," has been hospitable, and perhaps inspiring, to the genre's musicians: more jazz legends have lived here than anywhere else. Flushing Town Hall created this map as one of its myriad jazz programs, which include bus tours of the borough and a year-round performance and event schedule. The map also contributed to the establishment of Addisleigh Park as a U.S. historic district in 2011.

Map labels: TIMES SQUARE MOVIE THEATERS, USA SHAOLIN TEMPLE, MANHATTAN, ** BED-STUY, GZA, EAST NEW YORK, Brooklyn Bridge, Masta Killa, ODB, BROWNSVILLE, Verrazano Narrows Bridge, STAPLETON PROJECTS, NEW JERSEY, BROOKLYN ZOO, Ghostface Killah, RZA, PARK HILL* PROJECTS, Raekwon, U-God, Inspectah Deck, Method Man, Great Kills, SHAOLIN & ENVIRONS, SHAOLIN, Crooke's Point, * Never Ran Never Will, ** Do or Die

THE RZA and CHRIS NORRIS

Shaolin & Environs
From *The Wu Tang Manual*, 2005

The Wu-Tang Clan, an influential collective of independent hip-hop MCs that emerged from New York in 1993, drew inspiration from old kung fu movies and mined them for aliases, audio samples, and even guiding philosophies. RZA—a cofounder of the group and its de facto leader—named the Clan after a mythical sword that conferred invincibility on a posse of warriors, and he dubbed his Staten Island neighborhood "Shaolin" after a kung fu fighting style. *The 36th Chamber of Shaolin*, a 1978 kung fu classic, inspired the name of the group's first album. RZA wrote *The Wu-Tang Manual* as a guide to all things Clan, and included in it this map marking the roots of its original nine members, six of them from Staten Island.

RIGHT

ROB BEALS

Manhattan and the Bronx: The Official Birth of Hip Hop, 2010
Digitally rendered image

Rob Beals won a 2010 New York mapping challenge sponsored by the Cartographer's Guild (an online forum for creative mapmakers) with this map of locations that influenced the development of hip-hop. Very little about the places is documented, and many of them no longer exist. "These were the spots where early DJs and MCs set up turntables for parties and developed the genre," Beals says. Grandmaster Caz, from the Cold Crush Brothers, as well as others from various "old school" hip-hop forums, helped him pinpoint key locations. Beals creates maps as a hobby, mainly for strategy gaming sites.

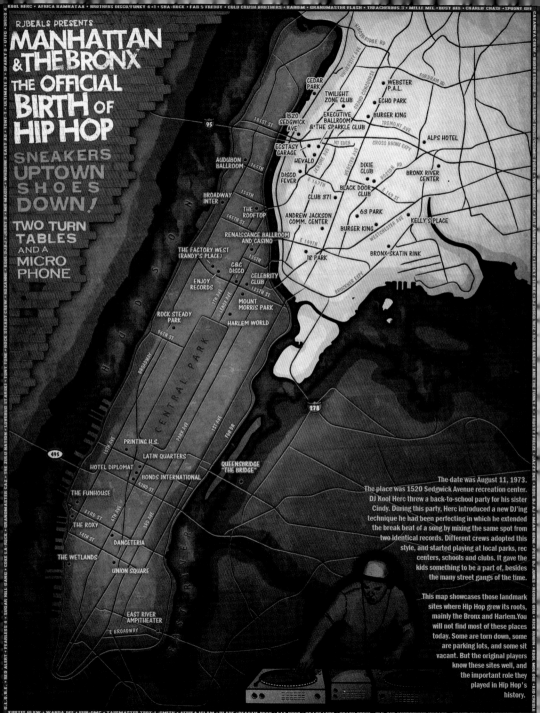

RJBEALS PRESENTS

MANHATTAN & THE BRONX
THE OFFICIAL BIRTH OF HIP HOP

SNEAKERS
UPTOWN
SHOES
DOWN!

TWO TURN
TABLES
AND A
MICRO
PHONE

The date was August 11, 1973. The place was 1520 Sedgwick Avenue recreation center. DJ Kool Herc threw a back-to-school party for his sister Cindy. During this party, Herc introduced a new DJ'ing technique he had been perfecting in which he extended the break beat of a song by mixing the same spot from two identical records. Different crews adopted this style, and started playing at local parks, rec centers, schools and clubs. It gave the kids something to be a part of, besides the many street gangs of the time.

This map showcases those landmark sites where Hip Hop grew its roots, mainly the Bronx and Harlem. You will not find most of these places today. Some are torn down, some are parking lots, and some sit vacant. But the original players know these sites well, and the important role they played in Hip Hop's history.

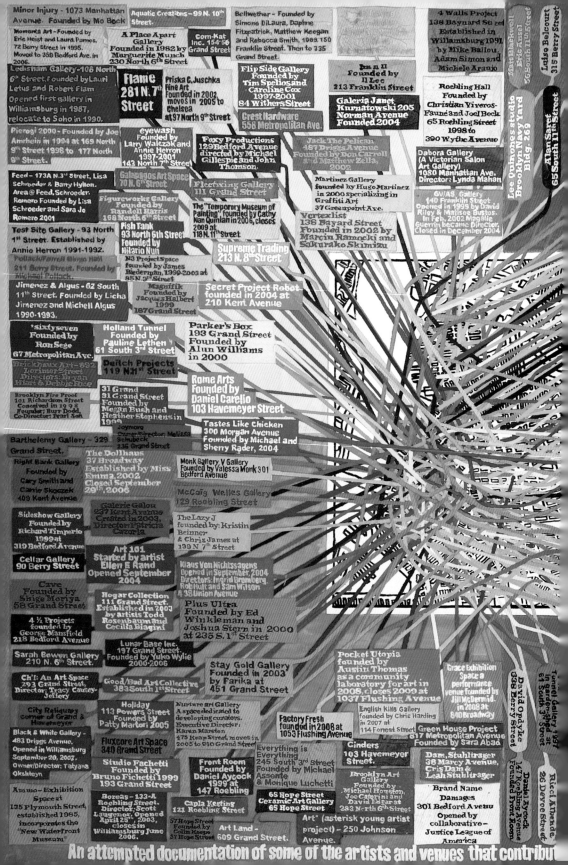

Minor Injury - 1073 Manhattan Avenue. Founded by Mo Beck

Momenta Art - Founded by Eric Heist and Laura Parnes, 72 Berry Street in 1995. Moved to 359 Bedford Ave. in 2006.

Ledisnam Gallery - 108 North 6th Street, founded by Lauri Letus and Robert Flam Opened first gallery in Williamsburg in 1987, relocate to Soho in 1990.

Pierogi 2000 - Founded by Joe Amrhein in 1994 at 169 North 9th Street 1998 to 177 North 9th Street.

Feed - 173A N.3rd Street, Lisa Schroeder & Barry Hylton. Area @ Feed, Schroeder-Romero Founded by Lisa Schroeder and Sara Jo Romero 2001

Test Site Gallery - 93 North 1st Street. Established by Annie Herron 1991-1992.

Pollack/Farrell Glass Hall 211 Berry Street. Founded by Michael Pollack.

Jimenez & Algus - 62 South 11th Street. Founded by Licha Jimenez and Michell Algus 1990-1993.

*sixtyseven Founded by Ron Sege 67 Metropolitan Ave.

Brickhaus Art - 892 Lorimer Street. Directors: Brian Hart & Debbie Joe

Brooklyn Fire Proof 101 Richardson Street. Conceived in 1993, Founder: Burr Dodd, Co-Director: Pearl Son

Barthelemy Gallery ~ 329 Grand Street.

Right Bank Gallery Founded by Cary Smith and Carrie Skoczek 409 Kent Avenue

Sideshow Gallery Founded by Richard Timperio 1999 at 319 Bedford Avenue

Cellar Gallery 90 Berry Street

Cave Founded by Shige Moriya 58 Grand Street

4 ½ Projects founded by George Mansfield 218 Bedford Avenue

Sarah Bowen Gallery 210 N. 6th Street.

Ch'I: An Art Space 293 Grand Street, Director; Tracy Causey-Jeffery

City Reliquary corner of Grand & Havemeyer

Black & White Gallery - 483 Driggs Avenue, Opened in Williamsburg September 20, 2002, Owner/Director: Tatyana Okshteyn

Ammo- Exhibition Space at 135 Plymouth Street, established 1985, incorporates the "New Waterfront Museum"

Aquatic Creations - 99 N. 10th Street.

A Place Apart Gallery Founded in 1982 by Marguerite Munch 230 North 6th Street

Corn-Kat Inc. 154/56 Grand Street

Flame 281 N. 7th Street

Priska C. Juschka Fine Art Founded in 2002 moves in 2005 to Chelsea at 97 North 9th Street

eyewash Founded by Larry Walczak and Annie Herron 1997-2001 143 North 7th Street

Galapagos Art Space 70 N. 6th Street

Figureworks Gallery Founded by Randall Harris 168 North 6th Street

Fish Tank 93 North 6th Street Founded by Hilario Nun

N3 Project Space founded by James Biederman, 1999-2003 at 85 N. 3rd Street

Magnifik Founded by Jacques Halbert 1999 187 Grand Street

Holland Tunnel Founded by Pauline Lethen 61 South 3rd Street

Deitch Projects 119 N. 11th Street

31 Grand 91 Grand Street Founded by Megan Bush and Heather Stephens in 1999

Seymore Owner/Director: Melissa Schubeck 236 Grand Street

The Dollhaus 37 Broadway Established by Miss Emma, 2002 Closed September 29th, 2006

Galerie Galou 237 Kent Avenue Created in 2003, Director Patricia Cazorla

Art 101 Started by artist Ellen E Rand Opened September 2004

Hogar Collection 111 Grand Street. Established in 2003 by artists Todd Rosenbaum and Cecilia Biagini

Lunar Base Inc. 197 Grand Street. Founded by Yuko Wylie 2000-2006

Good/Bad Art Collective 383 South 1st Street

Holiday 113 Powers Street Founded by Patty Martori 2005

Fluxcore Art Space 340 Grand Street

Studio Fachetti Founded by Bruno Fichetti 1999 193 Grand Street

Front Room Founded by Daniel Aycock 1999 at 147 Roebling

Boreas - 133-A Roebling Street. Director; Scott Laugenor. Opened April 18th, 2003, closes in Williamsburg June 2006.

Capla Kesting 121 Roebling Street

57 Hope Street Founded by Colin Lyons 57 Hope Street

Art Land - 609 Grand Street.

Bellwether - Founded by Simone DiLaura, Daphne Fitzpatrick, Matthew Keegan and Rebecca Smith, 1999. 150 Franklin Street. Then to 335 Grand Street.

Flip Side Gallery Founded by Tim Spelios and Caroline Cox 1997-2001 84 Withers Street

Crest Hardware 558 Metropolitan Ave.

Foxy Productions 129 Bedford Avenue directed by Michael Gillespie and John Thomson.

Electriciti Gallery 111 Grand Street

The "Temporary Museum of Painting," founded by Cathy Nan Quinlan in 2006, closes 2009 at 118 N. 11th Street

Supreme Trading 213 N. 8th Street

Secret Project Robot founded in 2004 at 210 Kent Avenue

Parker's Box 193 Grand Street Founded by Alun Williams in 2000

Rome Arts Founded by Daniel Carelio 103 Havemeyer Street

Tastes Like Chicken 300 Morgan Avenue Founded by Michael and Sherry Rader, 2004

Monk Gallery V Gallery Founded by Valessa Monk 301 Bedford Avenue

McCaig-Welles Gallery 129 Roebling Street

The Lazy J founded by: Kristin Beinner & Chris James at 199 N 7th Street

Klaus Von Nichtssagens Opened in September, 2004 Directors: Ingrid Bromberg, Rob Hult and Sam Wilson 38 Union Avenue

Plus Ultra Founded by Ed Winkleman and Joshua Stern in 2000 at 235 S. 1st Street

Stay Gold Gallery Founded in 2003 by Farika at 451 Grand Street

Nurture Art Gallery A space dedicated to developing curators. Executive Director: Karen Marston 475 Kent Street, moves in 2005 to 910 Grand Street

Factory Fresh founded in 2008 at 1053 Flushing Avenue

Everything is Everything 245 South 3rd Street Founded by Michael Assente & Monique Luchetti

65 Hope Street Ceramic Art Gallery 65 Hope Street

Art* (asterisk young artist project) - 250 Johnson Avenue.

Inn II Founded by Il Lee 213 Franklin Street

Galeria Janet Kurnatowski 205 Norman Avenue Founded 2004

Jack The Pelican 487 Driggs Avenue Founded by Don Carroll and Matthew Zella, 2002

Martinez Gallery founded by Hugo Martinez in 2000 specializing in Graffiti Art 37 Greenpoint Ave.

Vertexlist 138 Bayard Street Founded in 2002 by Marcin Ramocki and Sakurako Shimizu

Pocket Utopia founded by Austin Thomas as a community laboratory for art in 2006, closes 2009 at 1037 Flushing Avenue

English Kills Gallery founded by Chris Harding in 2007 at 114 Forrest Street

Cinders 103 Havemeyer Street.

Brooklyn Art Gallery Founded by Michael Hongson, Joe Cheuin and David Esgarat 283 North 6th Street

4 Walls Project 138 Baynard Street Established in Williamsburg 1991 by Mike Ballou, Adam Simon and Michele Araujo

Roebling Hall Founded by Christian Viveros-Fauné and Joel Beck 65 Roebling Street 1998 to 390 Wythe Avenue

Dabora Gallery (A Victorian Salon Art Gallery) 1080 Manhattan Ave. Director: Lynda Mahan

GV/AS Gallery 140 Franklin Street Opened in 1999 by David Riley & Matisse Bustos. In Feb. 2002 Magalie Guerin became Director. Closed in December 2004

Grace Exhibition Space a performance venue founded by Jill McDermid. in 2008 at 840 Broadway

Green House Project 617 Metropolitan Avenue Founded by Sara Abad

Dam, Stuhltrager 38 Marcy Avenue, Cris Dam & Leah Stuhltrager

Brand Name Damages 301 Bedford Avenu Opened by collaborative - Justice League of America

Matt Blackwell Eric Ansel 562 South 11th Street

Louise Belcourt 315 Berry Street

Lee Quinones studio Brooklyn Navy Yard Bldg. 269

Alan Saret 65 South 11th Street

Tunnel Gallery 1991 in garden shed at 61 South 3rd Street

David Opdyke 338 Berry Street

Daniel Aycock 147 Roebling Avenue Founded Front Room

Ricci Albende 26 Devoe Street

An attempted documentation of some of the artists and venues that contribu

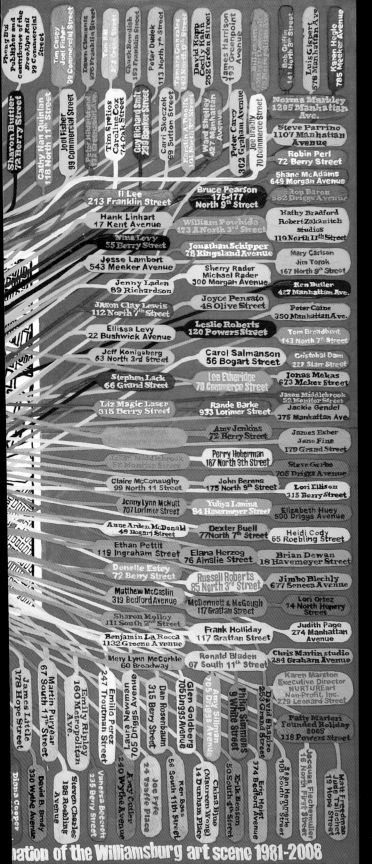

Phoey Bui
Publisher and
contributor of the
Brooklyn Rail
99 Commercial
Street

Tim Casey
Joel Fisher
99 Commercial Street

Dawn Clements
176 Franklin Street

Tom Hu
257 Green Street

Chuck Bowdish
163 Franklin Street

Peter Dudek
113 North 7th Street

Tamara Gonzales
43 North 8th Street

James Harrison
193 Greenpoint
Avenue

Bob Griffin
141 North 8th Street

Luis Gispert
576 Manhattan Ave.

Karen Hegle
785 Meeker Avenue

Sharon Butler
72 Berry Street

Cathy Nan Quinlan
118 North 11th Street

Joel Fisher
99 Commercial Street

Peter Hristoff
132 Greenpoint

Tim Spelios
Caroline Cox
174 Oak Street

Guy Richard Smith
239 Banker Street

Carri Skoczek
69 Sutton Street

Kerstin A. Roolfs
101 North 12th Street

Ward Shelley
427 Manhattan
Avenue

Peter Carey
302 Graham Avenue

Joe Bradly
70 Commerce Street

Norma Markley
1205 Manhattan
Ave.

Steve Parrino
1107 Manhattan
Avenue

Robin Perl
72 Berry Street

Shane McAdams
649 Morgan Avenue

Il Lee
213 Franklin Street

Bruce Pearson
175-177
North 9th Street

Roy Baron
562 Driggs Avenue

Hank Linhart
17 Kent Avenue

William Powhida
173 A North 3rd Street

Kathy Bradford
Robert Zakanitch
studios
119 North 11th Street

Nina Levy
55 Berry Street

Jonathan Schipper
78 Kingsland Avenue

Mary Carlson
Jim Torak
167 North 9th Street

Jesse Lambert
543 Meeker Avenue

Sherry Rader
Michael Rader
300 Morgan Avenue

Jenny Laden
89 Richardson

Joyce Pensato
48 Olive Street

Ken Butler
427 Manhattan Ave.

Jason Clay Lewis
112 North 7th Street

Leslie Roberts
120 Powers Street

Peter Caine
350 Manhattan Ave.

Ellissa Levy
22 Bushwick Avenue

Tom Broadbent
143 North 7th Street

Jeff Konigsberg
63 North 3rd Street

Carol Salmanson
56 Bogart Street

Cristobal Dam
227 Starr Street

Stephen Lack
66 Grand Street

Lee Etheridge
70 Commerce Street

Jonas Mekas
673 Meker Street

Jason Middlebrook
52 Monitor Street

Liz Magic Laser
315 Berry Street

Rande Barke
933 Lorimer Street

Jackie Gendel
375 Manhattan Ave.

Amy Jenkins
72 Berry Street

James Esber
Jane Fine
179 Grand Street

Jason Middlebrook
52 Monitor Street

Perry Hoberman
187 North 9th Street

Steve Gerbo
705 Driggs Avenue

Claire McConaughy
99 North 11 Street

John Berens
175 North 9th Street

Lori Ellison
315 Berry Street

Jenny Lynn McNutt
707 Lorimer Street

Yuliya Lanina
84 Havemeyer Street

Elizabeth Huey
500 Driggs Avenue

Anne Arden McDonald
49 Bogart Street

Dexter Buell
77 North 7th Street

Heidi Cody
65 Roebling Street

Ethan Pettit
119 Ingraham Street

Elana Herzog
76 Ainslie Street

Brian Dewan
18 Havemeyer Street

Donelle Estey
72 Berry Street

Russell Roberts
85 North 3rd Street

Jimbo Blechly
677 Seneca Avenue

Matthew McCaslin
319 Bedford Avenue

McDermott & McGough
117 Grattan Street

Lori Ortez
14 North Henery
Street

Sharon Molloy
111 South 2nd Street

Frank Holliday
117 Grattan Street

Judith Page
274 Manhattan
Avenue

Benjamin La Rocca
1132 Greene Avenue

Mary Lynn McCorkle

Ronald Bladen
67 South 11th Street

Chris Martin studio
284 Graham Avenue

James Little
178 Hope Street

Martin Puryear
67 South 11th Street

Emily Ripley
160 Metropolitan
Ave.

Emilio Perez
247 Troutman Street

Dan Rosenbaum
315 Berry Street

Laura Newman
705 Driggs Avenue

Glen Goldberg
705 Driggs Avenue

Amy Sillman
9 White Street

Philip Simmons
14 Dunham Place

David Shapiro
253 Grand Street

Karen Marston
Executive Director
NURTUREart
Non-Profit, Inc.
229 Leonard Street

Patty Martori
Founded Holiday
2005
118 Powers Street

Diana Cooper

David B. Brody
330 Wythe Avenue

Steven Charles
198 Roebling
Avenue

Vanessa Beecroft
235 Berry Street

Amy Cutler
240 Wythe Avenue

Joe Fyfe
24 Waffle Place

Ken Bass
56 South 11th Street

Erik Benson
50 South 4th Street

Eric Heist
374 Bedford Avenue

China Blue
(Maureen Wong)
14 Dunham Place

San Heisernich
108 South 11th Street

Jacques Flechemuller
16 North First Street

Julie LaChocher
15 Hope Street

Matt Friedman
178 Hope Street

...ation of the Williamsburg art scene 1981-2008

LOREN MUNK

An Attempted Documentation of Williamsburg, 2008–11
Oil on linen
60 x 72 in.

According to Loren Munk, this map documents only some of the artists and venues of Williamsburg's art scene from 1981 to 2008. He gave it a good shot, on a jam-packed five-by-six-foot canvas looking like a deconstructed rainbow of spaghetti. It's apparent that, compared with the mostly eponymous establishments of Manhattan, galleries are named more inventively here (Pocket Utopia, Factory Fresh, Everything Is Everything…). Just imagine all of the creative output produced in this little square of New York's map.

FOLLOWING PAGE

Concept by MARC H. MILLER, artwork by JAMES ROMBERGER and MARGUERITE VAN COOK, design by KEVIN HEIN

The East Village, New York City, 2001
Offset print based on ink and watercolor illustrations
24 x 18 in.

The beatniks brought the hippies, and the hippies brought the artists, writers, poets, musicians, actors, activists, and club owners. Cheap rents anchored the influential East Village scene of cultural ferment for more than three decades. The reverse side of this map from Ephemera Press provides descriptions of sixty-eight walking-tour sites, such as the former apartments of Abbie Hoffman, Robert Mapplethorpe, Diane Arbus, and Leadbelly; the studios of Joan Mitchell and Willem de Kooning; the site of Andy Warhol's *Exploding Plastic Inevitable*; and a mural by Keith Haring.

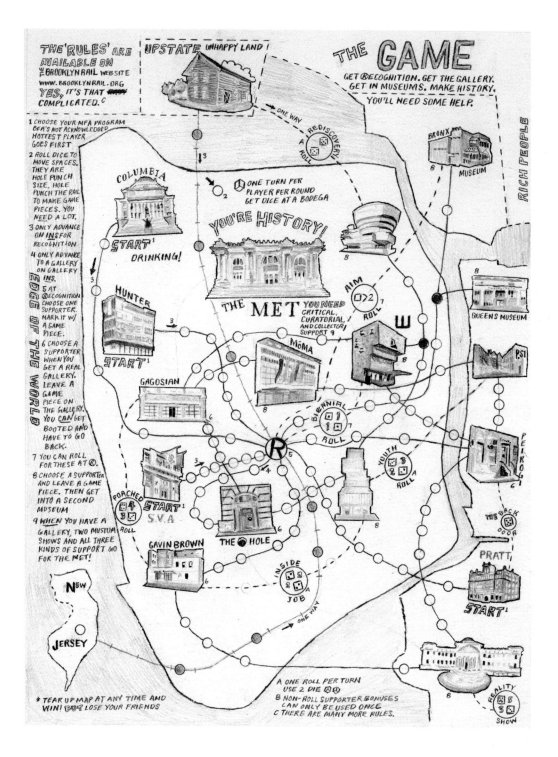

WILLIAM POWHIDA

The Game, 2010
One of two panels
Graphite on paper
30 x 23 in.

The goal of William Powhida's conceptual drinking game for artists is to get your work into the Met and make history. With each roll of the dice, "you will either go forward or backward, lose turns, or end up in New Jersey teaching." *The Game* is actually compellingly playable (go to Powhida's website for the detailed rules, including modifications for those who'd prefer to play "the bitter version"). Like the real art world, all you can do is create and solicit supporters (like James Kalm, the alter ego of Loren Munk; see page 196). And when given choices, make the right ones. The rest is just rolls of the dice.

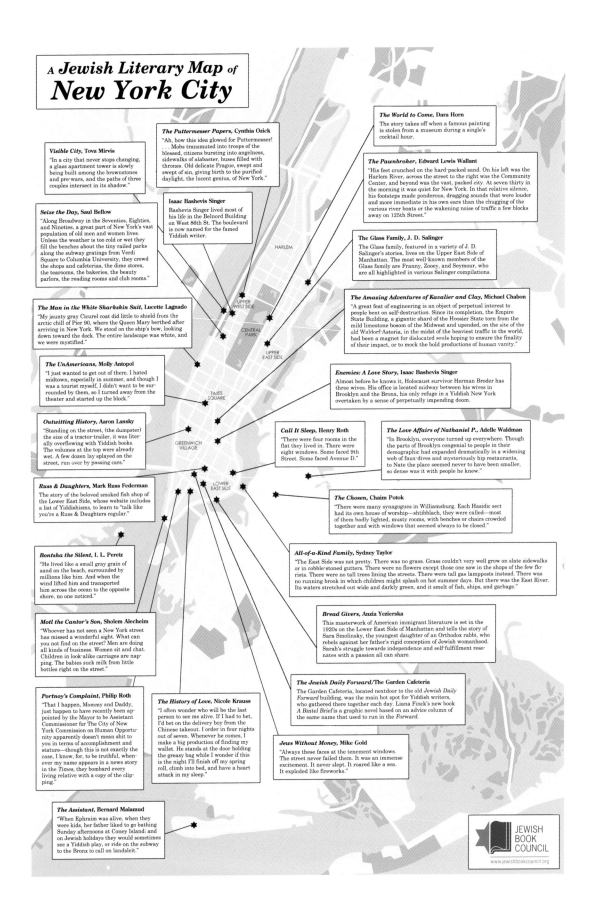

A *Jewish Literary Map* of
New York City

Visible City, Tova Mirvis

"In a city that never stops changing, a glass apartment tower is slowly being built among the brownstones and pre-wars, and the paths of three couples intersect in its shadow."

Seize the Day, Saul Bellow

"Along Broadway in the Seventies, Eighties, and Nineties, a great part of New York's vast population of old men and women lives. Unless the weather is too cold or wet they fill the benches about the tiny railed parks along the subway gratings from Verdi Square to Columbia University, they crowd the shops and cafeterias, the dime stores, the tearooms, the bakeries, the beauty parlors, the reading rooms and club rooms."

The Man in the White Sharkskin Suit, Lucette Lagnado

"My jaunty gray Cicurel coat did little to shield from the arctic chill of Pier 90, where the Queen Mary berthed after arriving in New York. We stood on the ship's bow, looking down toward the dock. The entire landscape was white, and we were mystified."

The UnAmericans, Molly Antopol

"I just wanted to get out of there. I hated midtown, especially in summer, and though I was a tourist myself, I didn't want to be surrounded by them, so I turned away from the theater and started up the block."

Outwitting History, Aaron Lansky

"Standing on the street, (the dumpster) the size of a tractor-trailer, it was literally overflowing with Yiddish books. The volumes at the top were already wet. A few dozen lay splayed on the street, run over by passing cars."

Russ & Daughters, Mark Russ Federman

The story of the beloved smoked fish shop of the Lower East Side, whose website includes a list of Yiddishisms, to learn to "talk like you're a Russ & Daughters regular."

Bontsha the Silent, I. L. Peretz

"He lived like a small gray grain of sand on the beach, surrounded by millions like him. And when the wind lifted him and transported him across the ocean to the opposite shore, no one noticed."

Motl the Cantor's Son, Sholem Alecheim

"Whoever has not seen a New York street has missed a wonderful sight. What can you not find on the street? Men are doing all kinds of business. Women sit and chat. Children in look-alike carriages are napping. The babies suck milk from little bottles right on the street."

Portnoy's Complaint, Philip Roth

"That I happen, Mommy and Daddy, just happen to have recently been appointed by the Mayor to be Assistant Commissioner for The City of New York Commission on Human Opportunity apparently doesn't mean shit to you in terms of accomplishment and stature—though this is not exactly the case, I know, for, to be truthful, whenever my name appears in a news story in *Times*, they bombard every living relative with a copy of the clipping."

The Assistant, Bernard Malamud

"When Ephraim was alive, when they were kids, her father liked to go bathing Sunday afternoons at Coney Island; and on Jewish holidays they would sometimes see a Yiddish play, or ride on the subway to the Bronx to call on landsleit."

The Puttermesser Papers, Cynthia Ozick

"Ah, how this idea glowed for Puttermesser! . . . Mobs transmuted into troops of the blessed, citizens bursting into angleness, sidewalks of alabaster, buses filled with thrones. Old delicate Prague, swept and swept of sin, giving birth to the purified daylight, the lucent genius, of New York."

Isaac Bashevis Singer

Bashevis Singer lived most of his life in the Belnord Building on West 86th St. The boulevard is now named for the famed Yiddish writer.

The History of Love, Nicole Krauss

"I often wonder who will be the last person to see me alive. If I had to bet, I'd bet on the delivery boy from the Chinese takeout. I order in four nights out of seven. Whenever he comes, I make a big production of finding my wallet. He stands at the door holding the greasy bag while I wonder if this is the night I'll finish off my spring roll, climb into bed, and have a heart attack in my sleep."

The World to Come, Dara Horn

The story takes off when a famous painting is stolen from a museum during a single's cocktail hour.

The Pawnbroker, Edward Lewis Wallant

"His feet crunched on the hard-packed sand. On his left was the Harlem River, across the street to the right was the Community Center, and beyond was the vast, packed city. At seven thirty in the morning it was quiet for New York. In that relative silence, his footsteps made ponderous, dragging sounds that were louder and more immediate in his own ears than the chugging of the various river boats or the wakening noise of traffic a few blocks away on 125th Street."

The Glass Family, J. D. Salinger

The Glass family, featured in a variety of J. D. Salinger's stories, lives on the Upper East Side of Manhattan. The most well-known members of the Glass family are Franny, Zooey, and Seymour, who are all highlighted in various Salinger compilations.

The Amazing Adventures of Kavalier and Clay, Michael Chabon

"A great feat of engineering is an object of perpetual interest to people bent on self-destruction. Since its completion, the Empire State Building, a gigantic shard of the Hoosier State torn from the mild limestone bosom of the Midwest and upended, on the site of the old Waldorf-Astoria, in the midst of the heaviest traffic in the world, had been a magnet for dislocated souls hoping to ensure the finality of their impact, or to mock the bold productions of human vanity."

Enemies: A Love Story, Isaac Bashevis Singer

Almost before he knows it, Holocaust survivor Herman Broder has three wives. His office is located midway between his wives in Brooklyn and the Bronx, his only refuge in a Yiddish New York overtaken by a sense of perpetually impending doom.

Call It Sleep, Henry Roth

"There were four rooms in the flat they lived in. There were eight windows. Some faced 9th Street. Some faced Avenue D."

The Love Affairs of Nathaniel P., Adelle Waldman

"In Brooklyn, everyone turned up everywhere. Though the parts of Brooklyn congenial to people in their demographic had expanded dramatically in a widening web of faux-dives and mysteriously hip restaurants, to Nate the place seemed never to have been smaller, so dense was it with people he knew."

The Chosen, Chaim Potok

"There were many synagogues in Williamsburg. Each Hasidic sect had its own house of worship—shtibblach, they were called—most of them badly lighted, musty rooms, with benches or chairs crowded together and with windows that seemed always to be closed."

All-of-a-Kind Family, Sydney Taylor

"The East Side was not pretty. There was no grass. Grass couldn't very well grow on slate sidewalks or in cobble-stoned gutters. There were no flowers except those one saw in the shops of the few florists. There were no tall trees lining the streets. There were tall gas lampposts instead. There was no running brook in which children might splash on hot summer days. But there was the East River. Its waters stretched out wide and darkly green, and it smelt of fish, ships, and garbage."

Bread Givers, Anzia Yezierska

This masterwork of American immigrant literature is set in the 1920s on the Lower East Side of Manhattan and tells the story of Sara Smolinsky, the youngest daughter of an Orthodox rabbi, who rebels against her father's rigid conception of Jewish womanhood. Sarah's struggle towards independence and self-fulfillment resonates with a passion all can share.

The Jewish Daily Forward/The Garden Cafeteria

The Garden Cafeteria, located nextdoor to the old *Jewish Daily Forward* building, was the main hot spot for Yiddish writers, who gathered there together each day. Liana Finck's new book *A Bintel Brief* is a graphic novel based on an advice column of the same name that used to run in the *Forward*.

Jews Without Money, Mike Gold

"Always these faces at the tenement windows. The street never failed them. It was an immense excitement. It never slept. It roared like a sea. It exploded like fireworks."

JEWISH
BOOK
COUNCIL

www.jewishbookcouncil.org

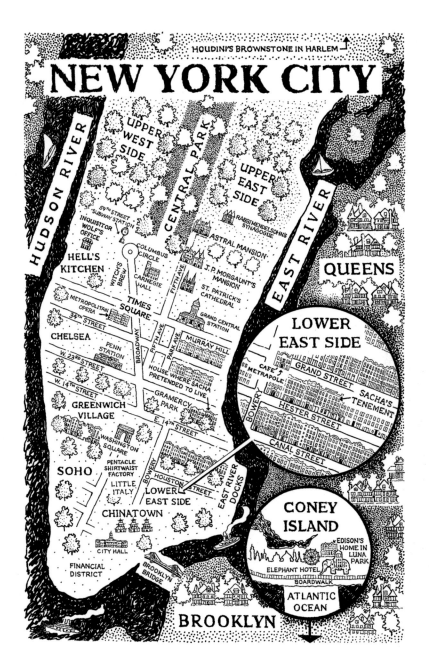

LEFT

DANI CRICKMAN

Jewish Literary Map of New York City, 2015
Printed poster from digitally rendered image

This map commissioned by the Jewish Book Council
features quotations from books by twenty-five writers. One
of them, from the 1930 novel *Jews without Money* by
Mike Gold, celebrates the entertaining street activity visible
from tenement windows. It gives an apt depiction of the city
overall: "It was an immense excitement. It never slept.
It roared like a sea. It exploded like fireworks."

MARK EDWARD GEYER

Title frontis illustration, *The Inquisitor's Apprentice*
by Chris Moriarty, 2011
Ink on vellum
14 x 8 in.

Mark Edward Geyer provided the illustrations for a series
of children's books portraying turn-of-the-century New York
as a place of ethnic mysticism and magic. This map is from
the first book in the series, in which the young protagonists
investigate the attempted murder of Thomas Edison.

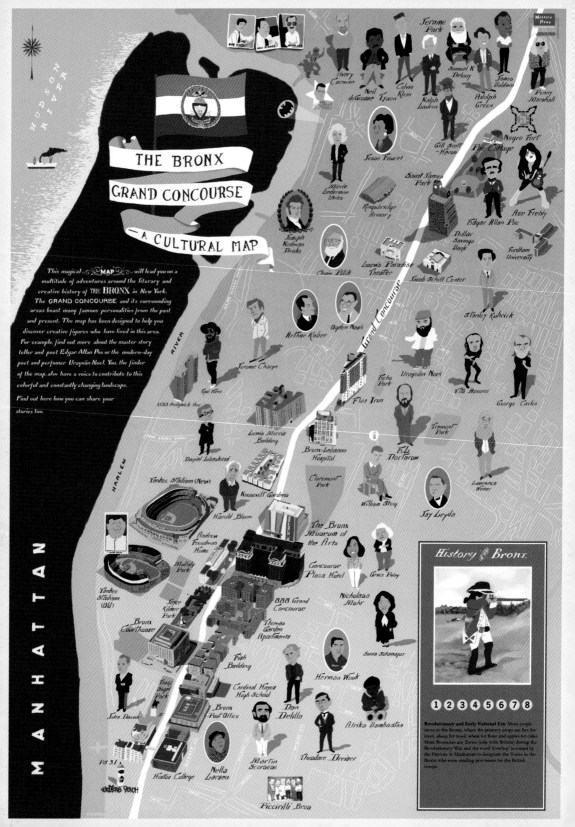

THE BRONX
GRAND CONCOURSE
— A CULTURAL MAP

This magical MAP will lead you on a multitude of adventures around the literary and creative history of THE BRONX in New York. The GRAND CONCOURSE and its surrounding areas boast many famous personalities from the past and present. The map has been designed to help you discover creative figures who have lived in this area. For example, find out more about the master story teller and poet Edgar Allan Poe or the modern-day poet and performer Urayoán Noel. You, the finder of the map, also have a voice to contribute to this colorful and constantly changing landscape.

Find out here how you can share your stories too.

History of the Bronx

1 2 3 4 5 6 7 8

Revolutionary and Early National Era: More people move to the Bronx, where the primary crops are flax for linen, sheep for wool, wheat for flour and apples for cider. Most Bronxites are Tories (side with Britain) during the Revolutionary War and the word 'Cowboy' is coined by the Patriots in Manhattan to designate the Tories in the Bronx who were stealing provisions for the British troops.

THE BRONX MUSEUM OF THE ARTS
Design by KEVIN WALDRON, research by TERRY WASSERMAN,
additional research and produced by TAMZIN BARFORD

The Bronx Grand Concourse—A Cultural Map (with details), 2013
Pencil and digital drawing
23 x 32½ in.

The four-mile-long Grand Concourse, built at the turn of the nineteenth century, was designed as the Champs-Élysées of the Bronx, a grand, tree-lined boulevard gracing the fast-growing borough. Find the Bronx Museum at no. 1040, and seek out the museum's online interactive version of the map to learn about the history of "the boogie-down borough" and its many illustrious denizens, past and present.

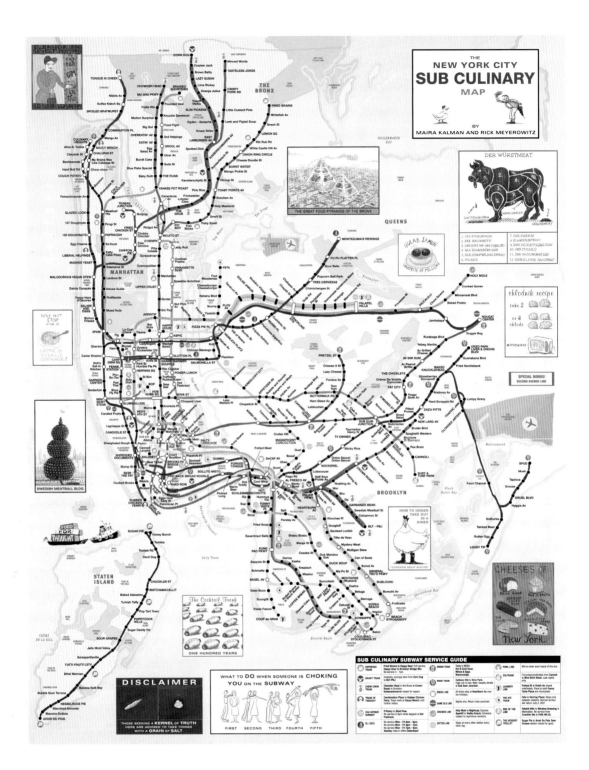

MAIRA KALMAN and RICK MEYEROWITZ
The New York City Sub Culinary Map (with detail), 2010
Digital print

In September of 2003, the idea for a food-related subway map came to Rick Meyerowitz as he headed downtown on an A train, absentmindedly thinking about lunch. Over the six years that followed, he and Maira Kalman conducted research for the project at ethnic food sources all over the

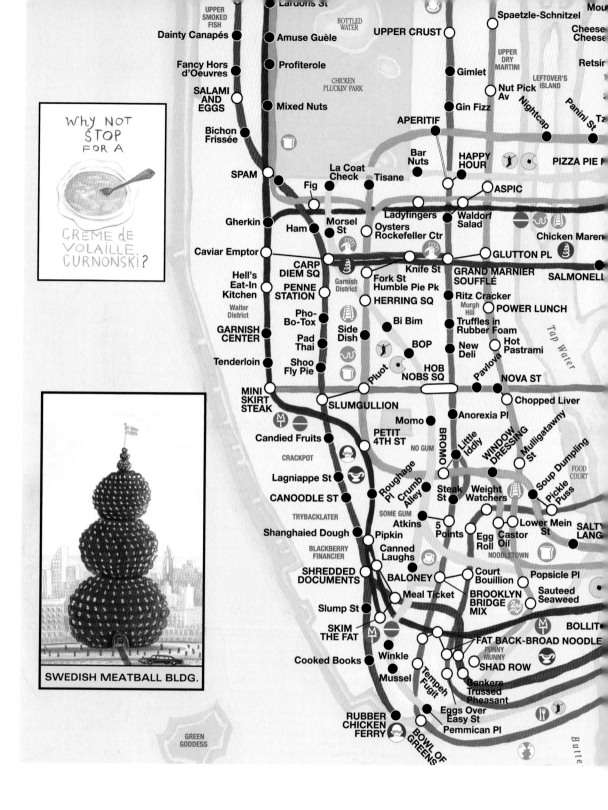

city. On a pencil sketch of the subway map, they assigned names to all 468 stations (adding sixteen for the Second Avenue line) and renamed all the neighborhoods, parks, cemeteries, and waterways—650 names in all. Meyerowitz painted a full-size subway map with all of the lines in place, and with Kalman added food-related illustrations. No doubt many New Yorkers would prefer to miss the stop for "Malodorous Vegan Stew" and proceed to "137 Doughnuts" (and thence to "Glazed Look").

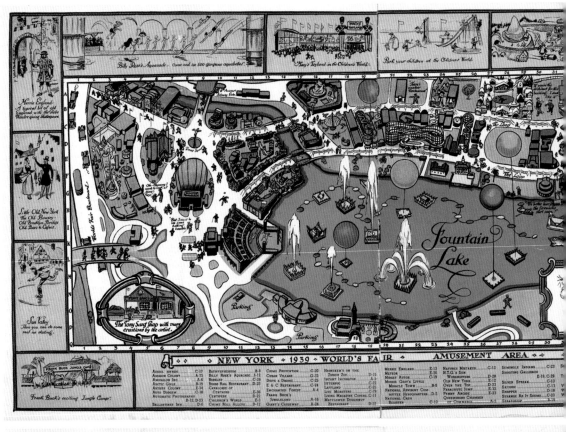

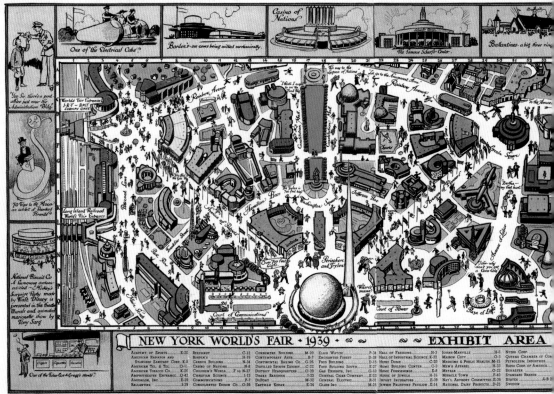

TONY SARG

New York 1939 World's Fair Amusement Area and *Exhibit Area*
From *The Official World's Fair Pictorial Map,* 1939
Courtesy David Rumsey Map Collection

Tony Sarg, a European emigrant, was many things to New York: a popular illustrator; the author of *Up & Down New York* (1926), a collection of lively scenes of the city; a star puppeteer; and the originator of the idea for parading giant inflatable floats down Broadway (Macy's first tried it out on Thanksgiving Day, 1928). Shown here, in two of six maps included in Sarg's wonder-filled pictorial atlas devoted to New York's 1939 World's Fair, are attractions by the score. In the amusement area fairgoers were diverted by midget autos, deep-sea dioramas, infant incubators, and a two-headed cow. The exhibition area featured such attractions as Miracle Town, the Hall of Fashions, the House of Jewels, and the Temple of Religion. And at the National Biscuit Co. Theater, visitors watched a humorous cartoon entitled "Mickey's Surprise Party" by Walt Disney, along with a marionette show by Tony Sarg himself.

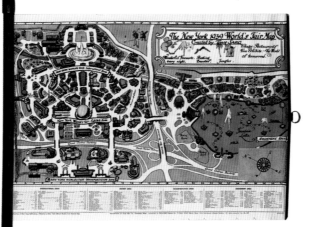

TONY SARG

New York 1939 World's Fair Cane Map, 1939
Wooden cane
36 in. height
Offset lithograph
13½ x 24 in.
Courtesy David Rumsey Map Collection

An ingenious invention for the multitasking fairgoer: a map that rolls out of a walking cane, for beating a path through the crowds. More than forty-four million people visited the New York 1939 World's Fair, over the course of two five-month seasons.

DAVID SULLIVAN

Coney Island 1905–06, 2015
Digital labels on scanned base map
10 x 18 in.

Because he is curious, David Sullivan knows a lot of interesting things about Coney Island. He was surprised to find no comprehensive historic map of the peninsula during its sixty years as the largest amusement center in the United States. To create a map for his website (Heart of Coney Island), Sullivan spent months researching and

Drawn By John G. Mark.

identifying almost two hundred locations from the resort's heyday of 1905–06, when three competing amusement centers (Luna Park, Steeplechase Park, and Dreamland) and a racecourse were entertaining millions of visitors. He relied on primary sources such as fire insurance maps, photographs, postcards, and advertisements to piece together an accurate picture of limitless thrills—overlaid on a 1906 map, *Bird's Eye View of Coney Island* by John G. Mark. Henderson's Music Hall was the last building standing from this era. It was close to the intersection of Surf and Stillwell Avenues, and was taken down around 2011.

MY CENTRAL PARK

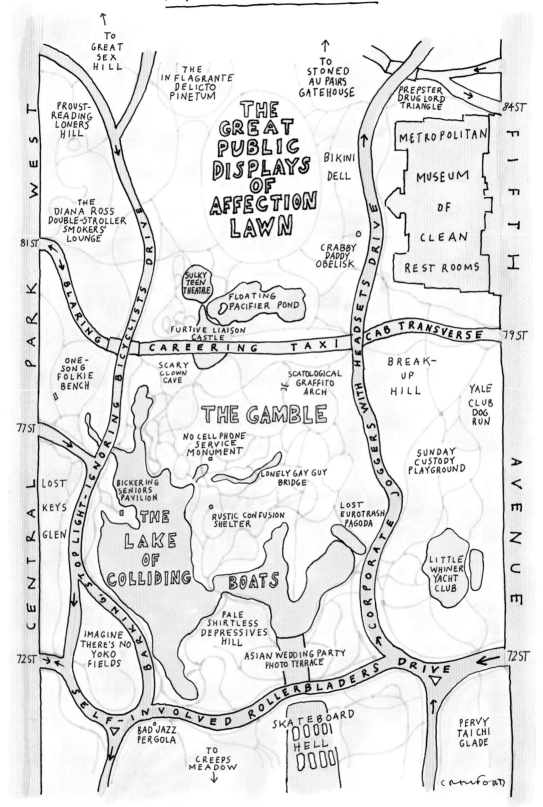

↑ TO GREAT SEX HILL

THE IN FLAGRANTE DELICTO PINETUM

↑ TO STONED AU PAIRS GATEHOUSE

PREPSTER DRUG LORD TRIANGLE

84 ST

PROUST- READING LONERS HILL

THE GREAT PUBLIC DISPLAYS OF AFFECTION LAWN

BIKINI DELL

METROPOLITAN MUSEUM OF CLEAN REST ROOMS

FIFTH

THE DIANA ROSS DOUBLE-STROLLER SMOKERS' LOUNGE

CRABBY DADDY OBELISK

81 ST

BLARING BICYCLISTS DRIVE

SULKY TEEN THEATRE

FLOATING PACIFIER POND

FURTIVE LIAISON CASTLE

CAREERING TAXI

CAB TRANSVERSE

JOGGERS WITH HEADSETS DRIVE

79 ST

ONE- SONG FOLKIE BENCH

SCARY CLOWN CAVE

SCATOLOGICAL GRAFFITO ARCH

BREAK- UP HILL

YALE CLUB DOG RUN

77 ST

PARK

CENTRAL

WEST

STOPLIGHT-IGNORING BARKING

THE GAMBLE

NO CELL PHONE SERVICE MONUMENT

LONELY GAY GUY BRIDGE

SUNDAY CUSTODY PLAYGROUND

LOST KEYS GLEN

BICKERING SENIORS PAVILION

RUSTIC CONFUSION SHELTER

LOST EUROTRASH PAGODA

CORPORATE

THE LAKE OF COLLIDING BOATS

LITTLE WHINER YACHT CLUB

AVENUE

IMAGINE THERE'S NO YOKO FIELDS

PALE SHIRTLESS DEPRESSIVES HILL

72 ST

SELF-INVOLVED ROLLERBLADERS DRIVE

ASIAN WEDDING PARTY PHOTO TERRACE

72 ST

BAD JAZZ PERGOLA

SKATEBOARD HELL

PERVY TAI CHI GLADE

↓ TO CREEPS MEADOW

crawford

LEFT

MICHAEL CRAWFORD

My Central Park, 2004
Ink and toner on paper
24 x 16 in.

More than six hundred of Michael Crawford's cartoons have appeared in the *New Yorker.* He is also an artist (he has done wonderful map paintings) and plays first base for the magazine's baseball team. There are no baseball diamonds on his Central Park map (the June 28, 2004 cover of the magazine), presumably so that little whiners, crabby daddies, and stoned au pairs won't find their way there.

JENNY ODELL

Satellite Collections: Every Outdoor Basketball Court in Manhattan, 2011
Digital print
24 x 24 in.

Jenny Odell's *Satellite Collections* portfolio looks like a dossier assembled by researchers on Planet X, puzzling over the identity of forms appearing on faraway planet Earth. Using Google Earth satellite imagery, the artist makes orderly collections of recurring features—empty parking lots, grain silos, swimming pools, nuclear cooling towers—that occur like landing pads over our landscapes. She found 116 baseball diamonds in Manhattan, and, for this piece, plucked dozens of basketball courts (woefully underused) from parks and lots throughout the island.

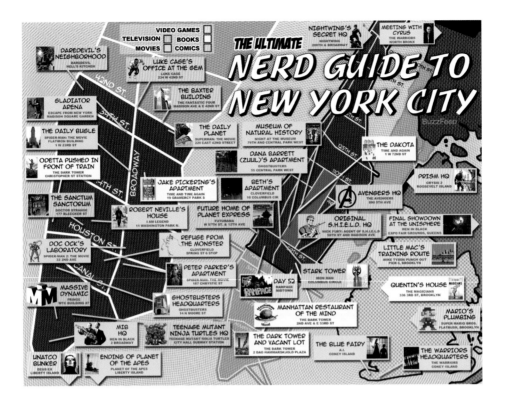

TANNER GREENRING and JACK SHEPHERD

The Ultimate Nerd Guide to New York City, 2011
Digitally rendered image

There are so many centers of altruism here:
the headquarters of Men in Black, the agents of
S.H.I.E.L.D., the Avengers, Teenage Mutant Ninja
Turtles. New Yorkers should feel well looked after,
with these guys watching our backs.

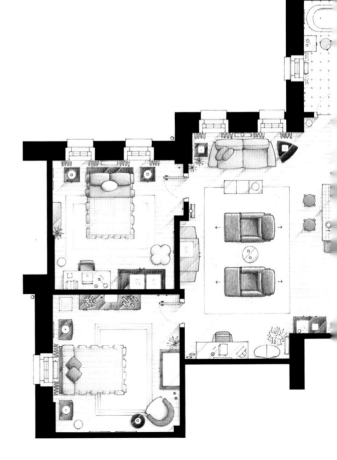

IÑAKI ALISTE LIZARRALDE

Apartments of Chandler + Joey and
Monica + Rachel, 2015
12½ x 16 in.
Colored pencil and marker on cardboard

This is a floor plan of apartments 19 and 20 at 495 Grove Street, the Greenwich Village clubhouse of six famous friends. But, as it turns out, that's a Brooklyn address. Enterprising fans found the real apartment building seen in the show's exterior shots at 90 Bedford Street, around the corner from Grove Street in the heart of the West Village. Iñaki Aliste Lizarralde is an interior designer in the Basque country of Spain who draws floor plans for relaxation and entertainment. At his Etsy store you can find wonderfully detailed drawings of the "homes" of other forever–New Yorkers: Carrie Bradshaw, Jerry Seinfeld, Holly Golightly, Will and Grace, and, of course, Lucy and Ricky.

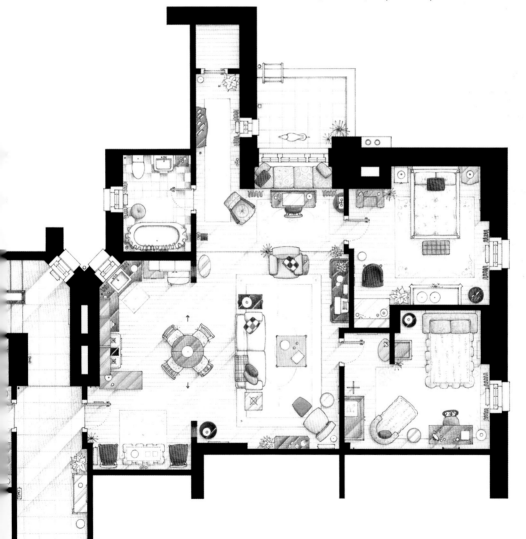

E. L. HARPER

*A Map of Manhattan Depicting Some Bright Spots
in That Dark Era Before the Saloon Left the Corner
and Moved Into the Home,* 1932

Color process print

16½ x 28¾ in.

Courtesy George Glazer Gallery

In 1932 Prohibition's repeal was just a year away, and to
whet the thirst of imbibers, this map looked back at the
halcyon, pre-1920 days when a bar or saloon in Manhattan
was never more than a stumble away. Ah, the good old

Morning to evening, weekdays and weekends, the Professional Paranormal Investigation & Elimination Authority is at your service, New York. Those in the know will recognize many references here—for example, Sebouillia Street is named for a largely unknown race whose lord was Gozer, and Torb Street refers to one of Gozer's known destructor forms. (We all know what Stay Puft Street is named for.) Even the subway line markers spell out messages in this thirtieth-anniversary commemorative print. The map is your resource if you ever notice something strange in your neighborhood.

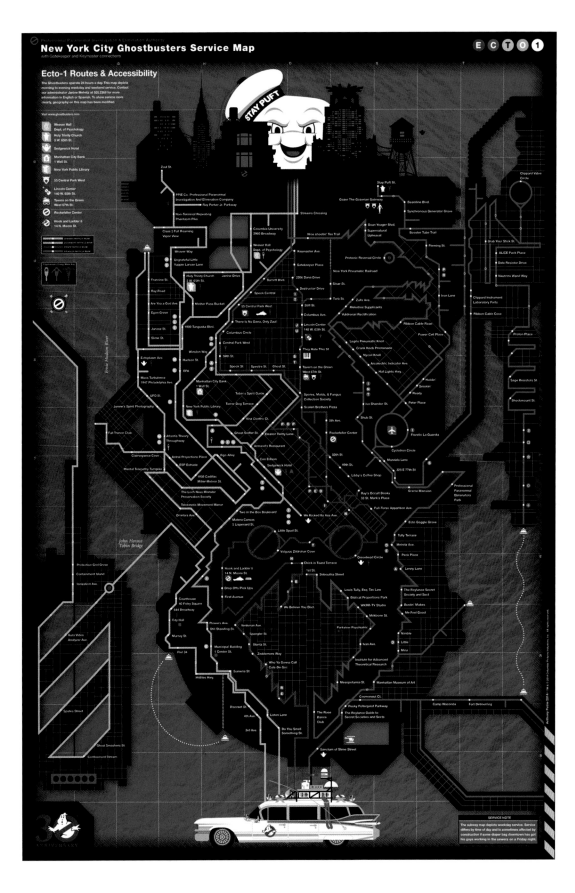

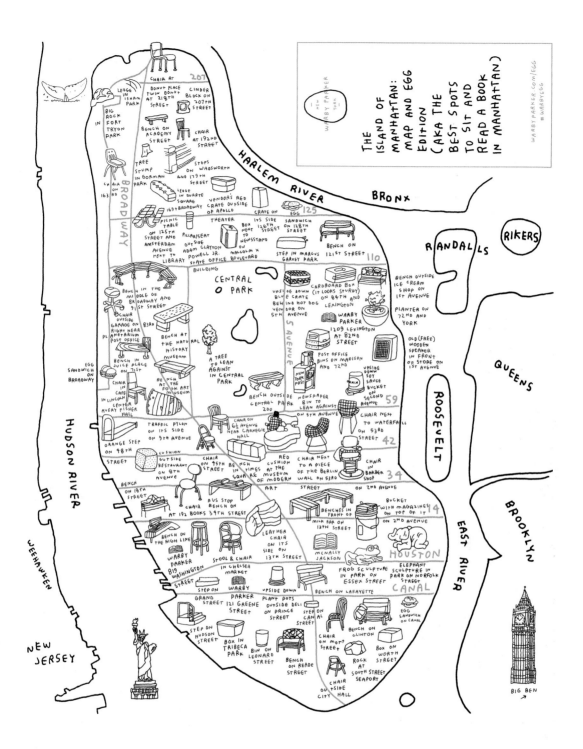

JASON POLAN

The Best Spots to Sit and Read a Book in Lower Manhattan, 2014

Folded map; original print on vellum
22 x 18 in.

Jason Polan is someone you want to hang out with, so entertaining are his various projects. For one thing, he'll draw you, as part of his Sisyphean goal to draw every person in New York (he has surpassed ten thousand). At an occasional meeting of the Taco Bell Drawing Club, he'll teach you how to draw a giraffe or an apatosaurus. You can pay him to handwrite your letter and digitize it, so that you can send someone a handwritten email. And you can ask him for his favorite Manhattan spot to sit and read, go there, and read his book *Every Piece of Art in the Museum of Modern Art*.

CHRISTO

The Gates (Project for Central Park, New York City), 2004
Drawing in two parts
Graphite, charcoal, pastel, wax crayon, aerial photograph,
fabric sample, and hand-drawn technical data
15 x 96 in. and 42 x 96 in.
Photo by Wolfgang Volz

For sixteen days in February 2005, New York experienced
an artistic installation by Christo and Jeanne-Claude that
was unprecedented in both scope and splendor. Some
7,503 gateways, spaced at twelve-foot intervals, straddled
Central Park's twenty-three miles of walkways. From each
hung a fabric panel, its weight ideal for billowing in a breeze.
Depending on the slant of the sun, the color of the banners
ranged from dark orange to a bright, glowing saffron.

The project had been in the making for twenty-five years.
It came to fruition with an alignment of circumstances—the
election of Mayor Michael Bloomberg, the near-completion
of a decades-long park restoration, and a city eager to bring
tourists back after the post-9/11 lull. The mayor's office
estimated that four million visitors entered the park during
the installation, 450,000 on its opening day alone. *The
Gates* sparked a voluble conversation about art for the public
in a public space—its purpose and its effects. What would
Olmsted and Vaux have said?

Despite the fabled nonchalance of Manhattanites, the
general mood in the park seemed one of awe and delight.
People crowded the roof of the Metropolitan Museum of
Art, strangers elbow to elbow, sharing impressions while
gazing at sinuous, orange-punctuated paths. When snow fell,
people boasted that they'd "seen it then," as vivid silhouettes
on a field of white. And each day throngs left the park with
small orange squares of fabric, handed out by volunteers—
souvenirs of a famously festooned Central Park.

7th. Avenue, Columbus Circle, Central Park West, Cathedral PKWY, West 110th. Street, 7500 gates along 23 mi. selected walkways

Bars 6"x12" x48' 160# weight 650-850 lb

Produced by:
Tributary Books

Published by:
Princeton Architectural Press
A McEvoy Group company
37 East Seventh Street
New York, New York 10003

Visit our website at: www.papress.com

Editor: Jenny Florence
Design: Jane Jeszeck, Jigsaw/www.jigsawseattle.com

Special thanks to: Madisen Anderson, Janet Behning, Nicola Brower, Abby Bussel, Erin Cain, Tom Cho,
Barbara Darko, Benjamin English, Jan Cigliano Hartman, Lia Hunt, Mia Johnson, Valerie Kamen,
Simone Kaplan-Senchak, Stephanie Leke, Diane Levinson, Jennifer Lippert, Kristy Maier, Sara McKay,
Jaime Nelson Noven, Esme Savage, Rob Shaeffer, Sara Stemen, Paul Wagner, Joseph Weston,
and Janet Wong of Princeton Architectural Press —Kevin C. Lippert, publisher

Library of Congress Cataloging-in-Publication Data
Harmon, Katharine A., 1960–
   You are here NYC : mapping the soul of the city / Katharine Harmon.
ISBN 978-1-61689-526-6 (alk. paper)
1. Cartography—New York. 2. New York—Pictorial works
LCC G1254.N4B7 H3 2016 DDC 912.747/1--dc23
LC record available at http://lccn.loc.gov/2016004560

LORDY RODRIGUEZ

Downtown, 2007

13 x 8 in.

Ink on paper

Collection of Fabio Rossi and Elaine Ng

Lordy Rodriguez likes to fiddle with maps, making the familiar unfamiliar in exuberant ways. Here he has imagined Manhattan with a canal in place of Canal Street and a wall in place of Wall Street.

The author extends much gratitude to all those who helped track down and/or provided images and permissions, and to the many who offered enthusiastic support over the past few years spent creating this book. Special appreciation goes to:

Rebekah Ashby-Colón, David Zwirner Gallery
Tamzin Barford
Nick Battis, Pratt Manhattan Gallery
BibliOdyssey.com
Daniel Blau, Daniel Blau Galleries
Bronx Museum of the Arts
Kevin J Brown, Geographicus Rare Antique Maps
Bridget Booher
Cliff Chanler
CityLab (.com)
Becky Cooper, New Yorker
Diana Ewer, TAG Fine Arts
Elizabeth Ferrer, BRIC
Melissa Flamson, With Permission
Jenny Florence, PAPress
George Glazer, George Glazer Gallery
Josh Hadro, New York Public Library Labs
Kris Harzinski, Hand Drawn Map Association
Janet Hicks, Artists Rights Society
Laura Hunt, Paula Cooper Gallery
Keith Lee Kroschel, Nu-Vue Studio
Laura Kuhn, John Cage Trust
Theresa Laughlin, TC Laughlin Public
    Relations Group
David Leopold, Al Hirschfeld Archives
Jennifer Lippert, PAPress
Stephen Lyons, Platform Gallery
Mapping New York (.com)
Charles Merguerian, Duke Geological Laboratory
Anne Mulherkar
New-York Historical Society
NY Curbed (.com)
Maria Popova, Brain Pickings (.org)
John Ptak, Science Books
Queens Museum
Jesse Roth, research services
David Rumsey, David Rumsey Historical Map
    Collection
Matt Singer, Warby Parker
Lenny Spiro, photographer
Nicola Twilley, Edible Geography; Gastropod
Untapped Cities (.com)
Kevin Waldron, Invisible Dog Art Center
Tim Wallace, *New York Times*

and especially

Jane Jeszeck, Jigsaw Seattle
Elizabeth Kaplan, Elizabeth Kaplan Literary Agency
John and Avery Fulford

Index

LOREN MUNK

Floor Plan of MoMA, 2012
Oil on linen
20 x 16 in.

Loren Munk is a New York artist with a limelight-grabbing
alter ego: James Kalm, a persona created in the mid-
nineties who has published hundreds of reviews and essays
in the *Brooklyn Rail* and other publications. "The Kalm
Report," filmed with a handheld camera and uploaded to
YouTube, takes viewers on audiovisual tours of New York art
exhibitions with Munk/Kalm as a guide. The project is part
criticism, part documentation, and part performance art, and
leaves time for Munk to pursue his own artistic output.

FOLLOWING PAGE

ANDY WARHOL

Untitled (Central Park Map with Compass), c. 1954
Gouache, ink, and graphite on paper, laid down on card
16½ x 11 in.
Courtesy Daniel Blau Munich

According to Andrew Blauner, the author of a book
on Central Park, Andy Warhol once said that it was
better to live in the city than in the country, because
in the city he could find a little bit of country, but
in the country there was no little bit of city. The
consummate New York artist produced several map
depictions of Central Park. In the park there is a
touching memorial to Warhol from his great friend
Charles Lisanby, an Emmy award-winning production
designer. A plaque inset in a stone reads, "For Andy,
whom I loved very much."

INSIDE BACK COVER

REBECCA RILEY

New York Metro, 2009 (detail)
Acrylic on paper
33 x 30 in.

Rebecca Riley's series of city paintings depicts urban
regions as living organisms, with the rate of cell division
correlating to density of development. Replicating cells
become ever-smaller units as city blocks divide into
buildings, buildings into apartments, apartments into
rooms. The DNA of the city appears both hyperactive
and resilient.